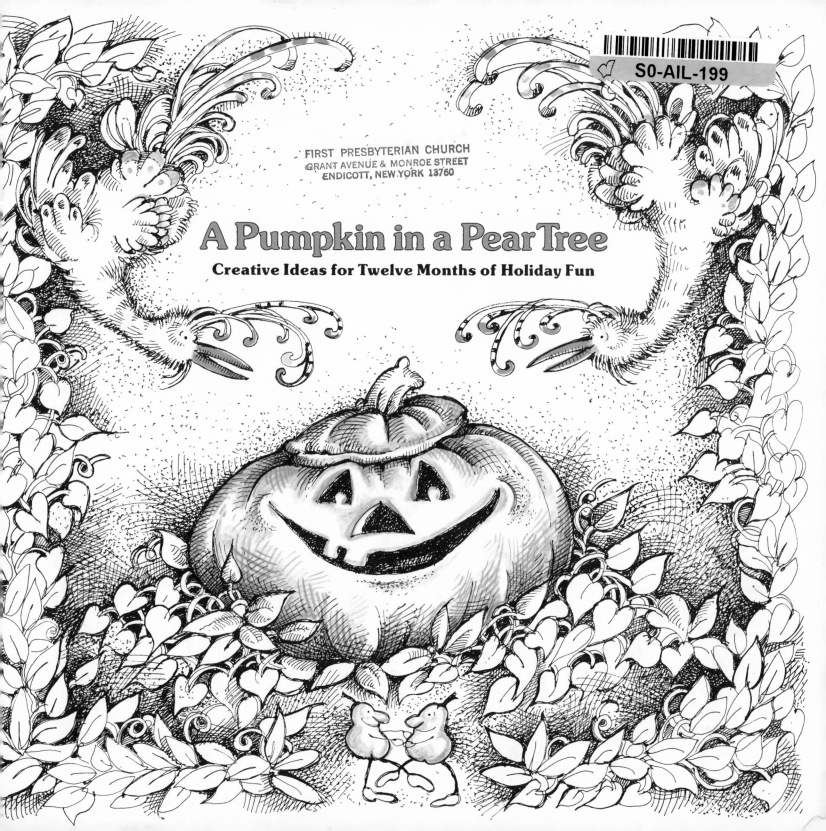

A Pumpkin in a Pear Tree

Creative Ideas for Twelve Months of Holiday Fun

A Pumpkin in a Pear Tree

Creative Ideas for Twelve Months of Holiday Fun

by
Ann Cole, Carolyn Haas,
Elizabeth Heller, and Betty Weinberger

Illustrated by Debby Young

LITTLE, BROWN AND COMPANY
Boston   Toronto

By Ann Cole, Carolyn Haas, and Betty Weinberger

I SAW A PURPLE COW
and 100 Other Recipes for Learning
(*with Faith Bushnell*)

A PUMPKIN IN A PEAR TREE
Creative Ideas for Twelve Months of Holiday Fun
(*with Elizabeth Heller*)

FIRST EDITION   T 03 / 76

*Published simultaneously in Canada
by Little, Brown & Company (Canada) Limited*

PRINTED IN THE UNITED STATES OF AMERICA

Library of Congress Cataloging in Publication Data

Main entry under title:

A Pumpkin in a pear tree.

Bibliography: p. 112
SUMMARY: Suggestions for simple projects, games, and crafts, using common household materials, for holidays throughout the year.

1. Handicraft — Juvenile literature. 2. Holiday decorations — Juvenile literature. 3. Cookery — Juvenile literature. 4. Games — Juvenile literature.
[1. Holiday decorations. 2. Handicraft. 3. Games.
4. Recipes] I. Cole, Ann. II. Young, Debby.
TT160.P85   745.59'41   75-17645
ISBN 0-316-15110-6

ISBN 0-316-15111-4 pbk.

To our parents . . .
because our enjoyment of the holidays started with you.

Clementine Reitman and Sylvester Flesheim (grandfather), Cleveland, Ohio (Ann)

Till and Michael Buhai, Bal Harbour, Florida (Carolyn)

Jane and Thomas Henkel, Kenosha, Wisconsin (Elizabeth)

Raye and Victor Kiralfy, Columbus, Georgia (Betty)

ACKNOWLEDGMENTS

We are grateful to the countless people who have given us their advice and expertise, including the staff members of the Chicago Public Library Information Service, the Field Museum of Natural History, the Adler Planetarium, and the many friends who shared their ideas for Martin Luther King Day and other holidays.

Special thanks go to Irene B. Feltes, our good friend and fellow worker, and to John G. Keller, our editor, for their patience, common sense, and good humor.

INTRODUCTION

Holidays are fun! Times for special treats . . . a pumpkin pie, a witch's brew, a mulligan stew. Times for special fun . . . a dance around the Maypole or an April Fools' Shoe Scramble.

Holidays have always been times of feasting, singing and dancing, and exchanging gifts, but they have a serious side, too, and understanding something about their true origins will help us to appreciate *how* and *why* each is celebrated. *A Pumpkin in a Pear Tree* offers a chance to sample a variety of ways to enrich our holiday enjoyment.

When the four of us set out to write a holiday book for children, we wanted to recreate the simpler, homespun holidays of our great-grandparents' era when close-knit families had to depend on their own resourcefulness. Many traditional pastimes — an old-fashioned taffy pull, an Easter egg roll, a neighborhood carnival — have found their way into our chapters, along with calico bows and strings of popcorn on the Christmas tree, colorful May baskets, and lacy, homemade valentines.

While researching the past, we naturally drew from our own childhoods and the special times we shared with our families and friends. However, in emphasizing the old, we have not overlooked today's new materials and innovations. Thus "Moonscapes," "Flip Dolls," and Styrofoam bonnets comfortably take their place beside time-worn traditions.

A Pumpkin in a Pear Tree is an imaginative activity book that, like its predecessor, *I Saw a Purple Cow,* features an easy-to-follow recipe format. The materials required are generally found around the house — egg cartons, cardboard tubes, margarine tubs, and the like. We have searched for activities that involve the whole family, bridging the generations by offering something for everyone, from toddlers to grandparents. In short, our approach

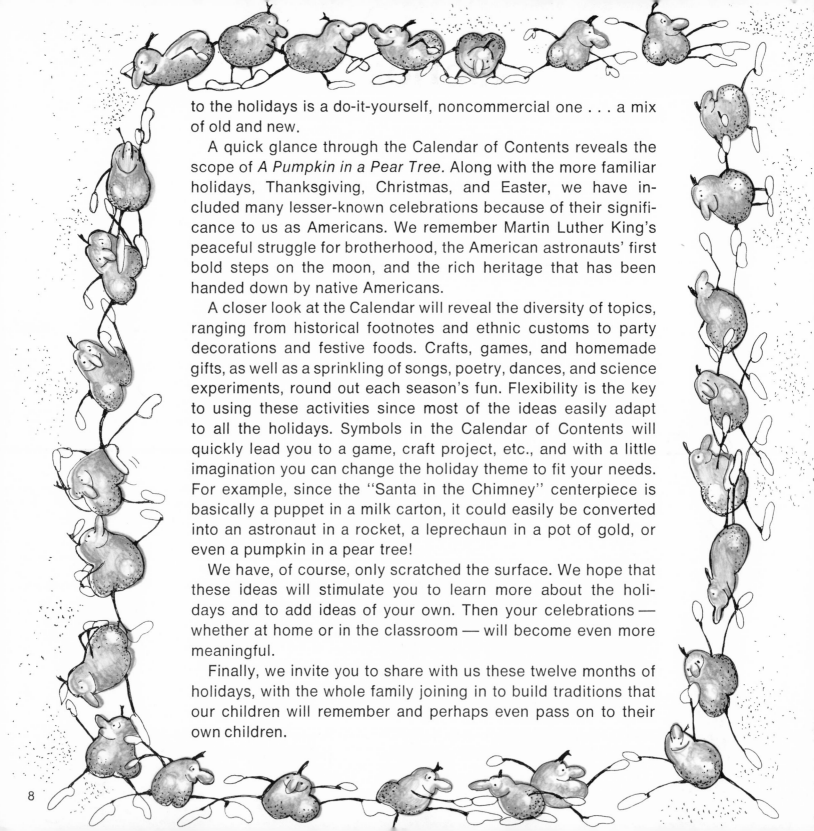

to the holidays is a do-it-yourself, noncommercial one . . . a mix of old and new.

A quick glance through the Calendar of Contents reveals the scope of *A Pumpkin in a Pear Tree.* Along with the more familiar holidays, Thanksgiving, Christmas, and Easter, we have included many lesser-known celebrations because of their significance to us as Americans. We remember Martin Luther King's peaceful struggle for brotherhood, the American astronauts' first bold steps on the moon, and the rich heritage that has been handed down by native Americans.

A closer look at the Calendar will reveal the diversity of topics, ranging from historical footnotes and ethnic customs to party decorations and festive foods. Crafts, games, and homemade gifts, as well as a sprinkling of songs, poetry, dances, and science experiments, round out each season's fun. Flexibility is the key to using these activities since most of the ideas easily adapt to all the holidays. Symbols in the Calendar of Contents will quickly lead you to a game, craft project, etc., and with a little imagination you can change the holiday theme to fit your needs. For example, since the "Santa in the Chimney" centerpiece is basically a puppet in a milk carton, it could easily be converted into an astronaut in a rocket, a leprechaun in a pot of gold, or even a pumpkin in a pear tree!

We have, of course, only scratched the surface. We hope that these ideas will stimulate you to learn more about the holidays and to add ideas of your own. Then your celebrations — whether at home or in the classroom — will become even more meaningful.

Finally, we invite you to share with us these twelve months of holidays, with the whole family joining in to build traditions that our children will remember and perhaps even pass on to their own children.

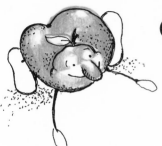

CALENDAR OF CONTENTS

Key:
C = Crafts
F = Food
M = Make-Believe

P = Presents
S = Science
AG = Active Games
TG = Table Games

These symbols identify those activities by category
that can easily be adapted to other holidays.

10

THE NEW YEAR

JANUARY 1

"Happy New Year"
Hang the new calendar high on the wall,
See Winter and Spring days
And warm days and colder.
One day is my birthday
Then I shall be older!

Johnell Manley, *Age 7*

Movable Dates

A Felt Board Calendar for Every Day of the Year

YOU NEED: a large piece of cardboard (poster-size)
felt (one large piece and several small pieces in contrasting colors)
scissors
felt markers
braid or rickrack
heavy yarn or twine
glue

YOU DO:

1. Cover the cardboard with felt.
2. Cut and label smaller felt squares and strips as follows: 31 numbered squares for the days; 1 long strip for days of the week; 12 strips for the months.
3. Glue on braid or rickrack for trim and attach yarn or twine for hanging.
4. At the beginning of each month change the name at the top and shift the numbers to the correct day of the week. (Glue a pocket onto the back to keep the extra months and dates.)

Chinese New Year

Ring out the old and ring in the new! People all over the world welcome in the New Year with parties, parades, general merry-making, and good intentions.

The Chinese, whose calendar is different from that used in the West, celebrate the day in midwinter with fierce lions and fire-eating dragons parading through the streets.

Line up your friends under a bedspread or sheet to make a

SCARY DRAGON

Put a huge *dragon mask* on the first one in line (to make a papier-mâché mask, see Halloween Masks, p. 81).

How many legs does *your* dragon have?

DRAGON TOYS

Tie spools, milk tops, and egg cups together with pipe cleaners or wire.

or

Cover the bumpy part of an egg carton (cut in half lengthwise) with a mesh potato sack, stuffing in a decorated paper cup for the head. Pinch shut with a twist top.

CHINESE LANTERNS

Strings of Chinese Lanterns light up the New Year. Here are three kinds you can make:

1. Cut out designs on a sheet of brightly colored paper. Roll into a cylinder and tape together at the seam.
2. Fold paper in fourths before cutting designs. Unfold and glue edges together forming a box shape.
3. Fold a piece of construction paper in half. Cut five or six slits through the folded edge, stopping about an inch from the top. Unfold and glue together lengthwise (slits will go up and down).

Attach paper handles for hanging in each case.

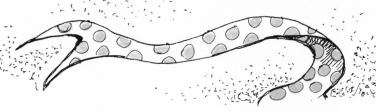

Welcome Pineapple

Many families traditionally have "open house" to greet their friends on New Year's Day. The early New Englanders showed their hospitality with a "Welcome Pineapple" filled with tiny gifts, one for each guest.

To make a papier-mâché pineapple centerpiece:

YOU NEED:
- a large balloon
- newspaper strips
- white glue (or wallpaper paste)
- water
- cardboard tube
- green construction or crepe paper
- tempera paint
- knife
- small wrapped gifts
- ribbons

YOU DO:
1. Blow up the balloon and tape a cardboard tube on the top for the stalk.
2. Cover the balloon and tube with strips of torn newspaper, dipped one at a time into a mixture of white glue and water. (Slide the strips through your thumb and finger to remove excess liquid.) Apply four or five layers, smoothing as you go, and let dry in a warm place overnight.
3. Cut off the top with a sharp knife (ask for help) and add long, pointed leaves to the stalk.
4. Next, paint the bottom to look like a pineapple.
5. Before putting the small wrapped gifts inside your pineapple, tie a *long* ribbon to each one.
6. Now place your centerpiece on the table, with a ribbon running from it to each place setting.

MARTIN LUTHER KING'S BIRTHDAY JANUARY 15

"I have a dream that one day . . . the sons of former slaves and the sons of former slave owners will be able to sit down together at the table of brotherhood. . . . I have a dream that my four little children will one day live in a nation where they will not be judged by the color of their skin but by the content of their character."
— *Martin Luther King, March on Washington, August 28, 1963.*

On Martin Luther King's Birthday you might, as a family, share your thoughts about these prophetic words and try to appreciate the meaning behind all that he struggled for.

"If My Three Dreams Came True"

Take turns discussing your dreams or wishes for making the world a better place for everyone to live, and talk about ways you might try to start making those dreams come true.

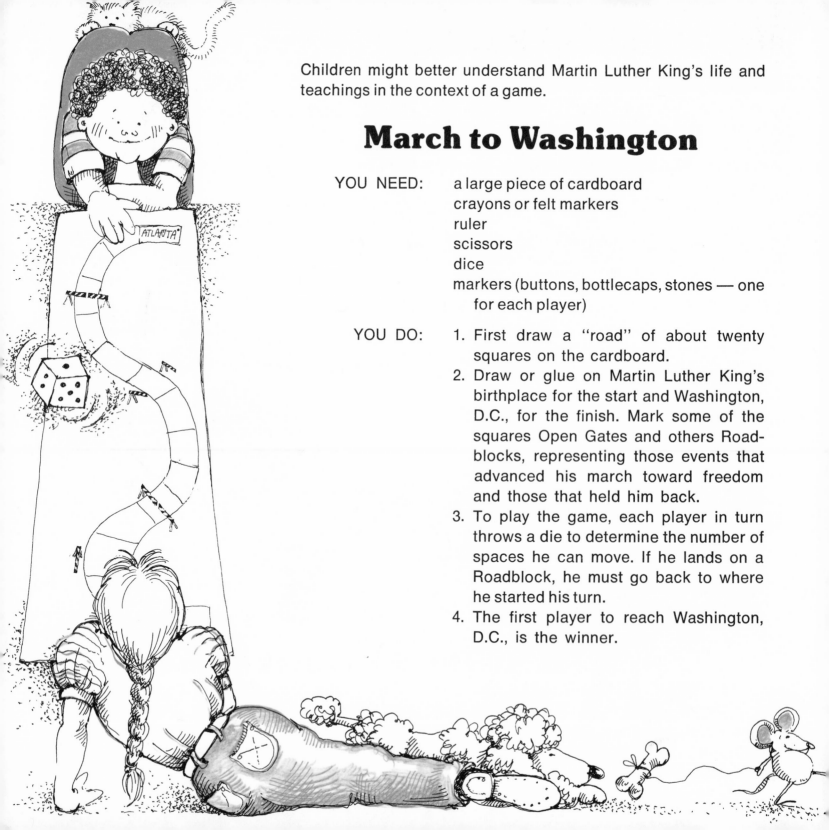

Children might better understand Martin Luther King's life and teachings in the context of a game.

March to Washington

YOU NEED:
a large piece of cardboard
crayons or felt markers
ruler
scissors
dice
markers (buttons, bottlecaps, stones — one for each player)

YOU DO:
1. First draw a "road" of about twenty squares on the cardboard.
2. Draw or glue on Martin Luther King's birthplace for the start and Washington, D.C., for the finish. Mark some of the squares Open Gates and others Road-blocks, representing those events that advanced his march toward freedom and those that held him back.
3. To play the game, each player in turn throws a die to determine the number of spaces he can move. If he lands on a Roadblock, he must go back to where he started his turn.
4. The first player to reach Washington, D.C., is the winner.

Older children might do some research and try to identify some Open Gates and Roadblocks that actually confronted King in his lifetime.

You could also use this information to design cards for a concentration game.

Concentrate on King

First divide 20 to 24 cards into four equal sets:

On one set of cards mark Roadblocks (−).

On the second set mark Open Gates (+).

On the third, write some obstacles that blocked King and his followers. Examples: Blacks required to sit in the back of the bus. Must pay poll tax to vote.

On the last set, use situations that furthered his cause. Examples: Peaceful march on Selma. Lunch counter sit-ins.

Then lay the cards on the table face down and proceed as in the game of Concentration, trying to make pairs by matching Roadblocks (−) with obstacles and Open Gates (+) with success situations.

FEBRUARY

VALENTINE'S DAY FEBRUARY 14

Valentine's Day combines two celebrations, one pagan, the other Christian. Originally, the Romans honored Lupercus (the god who kept the wolves away) on February 15 with a lovers' festival called Lupercalia. Each young man drew the name of a girl from a box to find his partner for the romantic celebration. Later, (A.D. 496) the pope established the fourteenth of February as the feast day of Saint Valentine, the martyred priest of the third century who gave aid and comfort to persecuted Christians.

The custom of sending love messages grew out of the notion that February 14 was the first day of the birds' mating season. We still send valentines to those we love, bedecked with hearts and cupids.

Old-Fashioned Valentines

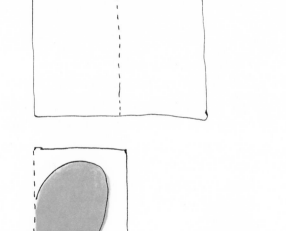

YOU NEED: construction paper (pink, red, white)
foil (silver, gold, red)
scraps of wrapping paper and fabric (especially small prints, ginghams, and checks)
trim: doilies, braid, rickrack

YOU DO:

1. Practice making a heart by folding a square of paper in half and cutting it as shown (start cutting at bottom left corner). How many smaller hearts can you cut from one large heart?
2. Arrange and glue all your hearts on a contrasting sheet of construction paper. For a really old-fashioned look, add lace doilies, rickrack, braid, and other trim.
3. Now write your message and send it to a very special person.

Valentines with a New Look

"BROKEN HEART" PUZZLE

Make a large heart from construction paper. Decorate the front with crayons or felt markers and then write a love note on the back. Cut the heart into several pieces and put them in an envelope. Some silly messages are: Mend My Heart, Don't Break My Heart, Let's Get Together, I Go to Pieces over You.

LOVE-A-GRAM

Cut out letters and words from magazines or newspapers, choosing varied print sizes and styles. Arrange the letters into words, phrases, or sentences and glue onto a card. It's also fun to combine words or individual letters with pictures to spell out your message.

TISSUE COLLAGE

Cut out hearts and other valentine shapes (cupids, arrows, flowers) from various colors of tissue paper. Using a brush, first cover the front side of a folded piece of construction paper with a mixture of glue thinned with water. Next lay on several shapes (overlapping some) and smooth them down with your hand. Make several layers, brushing glue over each one. Then add a message on the inside.

STENCILS

Cut a heart shape out of cardboard, giving you *two* stencils. Place either stencil on paper and with colored chalk or crayon gently rub *over* the open one and trace *around* the solid one. You can make an interesting valentine design by moving the stencils around the paper.

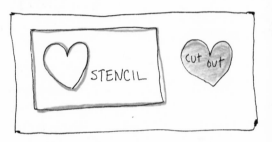

SPATTER

Using the same stencils, substitute paint for the chalk. Spatter the paint *through* a screen held directly over the stencil. An old toothbrush is handy for this process.

PULL-A-PRINT

First cut away the edges of a Styrofoam food tray. Then draw a picture on the tray, pressing down hard with a pencil or ballpoint pen. Cover the tray with one or more colors of tempera paint (not too thin). Next, place a piece of paper over the painted surface, rub gently, and presto! you have a print or copy of your picture. (If you add words to your design, be sure to write backwards.)

You can use these same ideas for other holiday cards: New Year's, Easter, Mother's Day and Father's Day, Chanukah, and Christmas.

thick paint

Special Places for Your Valentines

Make a **VALENTINE TRAIN** by stringing together boxes of various sizes and shapes. Shoeboxes and milk and oatmeal cartons work well. Cover them with construction paper, adding a cardboard tube smokestack, paper windows and doors, and button, spool or jar lid wheels. Label each "car" with someone's name for "incoming" valentines or use the train to sort your "outgoing" valentines according to their destination: For School, For Home, For the Neighborhood, For the Post Office.

Build a **PRETEND POST OFFICE** from a large packing box. Cut out a door and several windows and fold back a counter. Make openings for mail slots and label them Local, Air Mail, and Special Delivery. (Be sure to tape a shoebox behind each slot to catch the letters.) Have pretend stamps and money on hand for your "customers" and perhaps even a scale for weighing larger valentines and packages.

Make a **MAILBOX** out of a large cereal box or oatmeal carton. Cut out a flap for a mail chute, then decorate in blue and red to resemble a real mailbox.

To deliver the valentines yourself, make a **MAIL POUCH** from a shopping bag or sturdy cloth. Attach an old belt or rope for a shoulder strap (or use a backpack, if you have one).

A Royal Valentine Party

"Calling all Kings, Queens, and Jacks. By royal proclamation, you are invited to our castle for a regal costume party."

The King (or Queen) of Hearts

PAPER CROWN, THRONE, SCEPTRE

Make a paper crown from a wide band of construction paper, taped or clipped together in the back. Glue on hearts, "jewels," foil, glitter, or other fancy trim for a regal look. For a throne, cover a chair with an old sheet or tablecloth and decorate it with a Valentine motif, using crepe paper, ribbons, etc. Wrap crepe paper or foil around a long coat-hanger tube and glue two hearts back-to-back at the top; this will be your "ruling" sceptre.

"The Queen of Hearts, she made some tarts, all on a summer's day . . ."

TARTS

YOU NEED:
1 cup flour
⅓ cup plus 1 tablespoon shortening
2 tablespoons water
pinch of salt

YOU DO: Cream the flour and shortening together. Add the water and salt and mix well. Roll into small balls. Press down into muffin tins with your thumb. Bake 8 to 10 minutes at 350°. Cool and fill with raspberry, strawberry, or cherry preserves. Add nuts, raisins, or powdered sugar, if you wish.

All of your guests will surely "steal" these tarts away!

Make a **SERVING TRAY** for your tarts by covering a box lid with foil and decorating it with red hearts and paper lace doilies. Loop a long ribbon or yarn through a hole in each side of the lid to hang around your neck.

Bake **VALENTINE CUPCAKES** by following the directions for a prepared cake mix. Frost with pink or white icing and add candy hearts, red hots, or gumdrops. *Stencil* on a heart by cutting a heart shape from lightweight cardboard. Place the stencil over the iced cupcakes one at a time and sprinkle on red sugar.

Serve your tarts or cupcakes with a **PRINCESS PUNCH**. Mix a red fruit drink with lemon-lime soda and float raspberry sherbet on top, *or* let frozen raspberries or strawberries thaw and then combine with milk; stir well, and top with whipped cream and cherries.

VALENTINE CASTLE

Turn your cake mix box, along with other small boxes, milk cartons, and cardboard tubes into a royal centerpiece. Cover with construction paper, tissue paper, or foil. Put on a cardboard or paper roof, doors, and windows. Add watchtowers made from cardboard tubes. Top the castle with banners attached by toothpicks and trim with lace doilies, ribbons, and crepe paper.

THRONE GAME

The players are: the Queen of Hearts who sits on her throne, the Knave who tries to steal a tart, and the remaining guests (the royal courtiers) who are standing on red construction-paper "tarts" (bases). Whenever the Queen calls, "All change places," everyone must scramble for a new base while the Knave tries to steal one away. Whoever is left without a base becomes the new Knave. Players take turns being the Queen.

23

PRESIDENTS' BIRTHDAYS

Two of our most famous presidents, George Washington, the first, and Abraham Lincoln, the sixteenth, were born in February. Lincoln's birthday falls on the twelfth and Washington's on the twenty-second, but the latter is now celebrated as a federal holiday on the third Monday of the month.

Although they came from very different backgrounds (Washington grew up on a Virginia plantation, while Lincoln began his life in a humble Kentucky cabin), there are many parallels in their lives. (Washington's strategy during the Revolutionary War had a strong influence on the young Abe Lincoln, who read about it in one of his favorite books, *The Life of Washington* by Weems.)

Both presidents believed in the ideals of freedom and equality. Despite the fact that he had inherited slaves, Washington provided in his will for their freedom; sixty-four years later, during the Civil War, Lincoln issued the Emancipation Proclamation.

Lincoln Log Cabin

Lincoln's first home was a simple log cabin on the Kentucky prairie. Recreate a Lincoln Log Cabin with a milk carton or box as a base. Leave openings for the windows and doors. Add a chimney and roof to complete the cabin.

Three different ways to make the logs:
1. A simple method: Cover the carton with construction paper and draw on "logs".
2. For a three-dimensional look: Roll brown paper (grocery bags are handy) into tubes. Glue them onto the carton.
3. For an authentic look: Glue on twigs, painted straws, or popsicle sticks.

or bake a
Lincoln Log Cake

Follow the directions on a devil's food cake mix and then bake it in a greased coffee can. Swirl the frosting and add chocolate sprinkles, toasted coconut, or coarsely chopped peanuts to look like bark.

For George Washington's birthday add cherries and a paper hatchet to your log cake.

Shadow boxes are fascinating because they give a miniature, three-dimensional view which makes any scene, even one of long ago, seem almost real.

Washington's Peek Box

YOU NEED: a shoebox with a lid
construction paper
glue
tape
scissors
cellophane or tissue paper

YOU DO:

1. Cut out construction paper shapes of people and objects that remind you of George Washington (as a young boy, a general, or later as President).
2. Fold each figure ½ inch from the bottom and glue or tape the folded tab to the bottom of the box. (You can also color or glue scenery on the sides and back of the box.)
3. Cut a large rectangular opening in the lid. Cover it with colored cellophane or tissue paper glued to the underside. Then place the lid on the box.
4. Cut a "peek hole" the size of a half-dollar at the front of the shoebox to view a miniature scene.

What would you put in Lincoln's peek box?

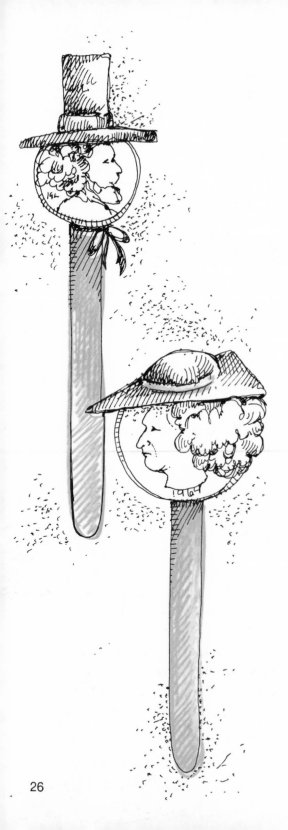

Stick Puppets

Many books have been written about these two great leaders and provide background for dramatizing the important events of their lifetimes. Use simple stick puppets to act out their stories.

YOU NEED: a Lincoln penny or Washington quarter
a clothespin or a Popsicle stick
scissors
glue
masking tape
yarn
cotton
construction paper
cloth scraps

YOU DO:
1. Use the coin for the face and glue it to the top of a clothespin or stick.
2. Then dress your puppet to look like one of the Presidents. Add cotton or yarn for hair and beard; use cloth or construction paper to make a tall hat and a bow tie for Lincoln and a "tricornered" hat for Washington.

For a party or classroom group activity, give everyone a paper bag filled with the items needed to create a puppet. Put a name on each bag and tie it with red, white, and blue or other brightly colored yarn or ribbon.

Presidential Coins

Make some giant presidential coins from aluminum pie tins. Using a Popsicle stick, push in a design from the back, remembering to reverse all the lettering! You can also cover a coin with foil and rub it until the design comes through.

Plaster Medallions

Mix plaster of Paris and water to a medium consistency in an empty can. Pour ¼ to ½ inch of plaster into a small plastic-coated drinking cup. Quickly poke a straw through the plaster *near* the edge to make a hole for hanging. When dry, peel away the cup, remove the straw, and carve or paint your medallion to resemble your favorite president.

Pitching Pennies

Try pitching pennies into a milk carton decorated to look like a Lincoln top hat or pitch them across the Delaware. (Use a scarf or rug for the river.) Back up a step each time to make the game more challenging.

George Washington dreamed of becoming a sailor while he was growing up on a tobacco plantation, but his father died when he was a young boy, and he had to learn a trade instead. At the age of fourteen, he left home to live with his brother, Lawrence, at Mount Vernon, where he became a surveyor.

Mental Measuring — a "surveying" game

1. One child plays "surveyor" and holds up a stick, pencil, cardboard, or other straight object.
2. The other children look carefully at the object to "memorize" its length.
3. Next, each child (with his two index fingers) marks off a place in the room that he thinks is exactly the same length as the stick (a table leg, picture frame, windowpane, etc.). Then the "surveyor" places his measuring stick against each player's marked-off spot. Whoever made the best mental measurement becomes the surveyor for the next round and selects *another* straight object of a different length.

Variations. Ask the players to guess the actual length of the "surveyor's" stick. Using a ruler, measure to see whose estimate is the most accurate. Can you guess the length in decimeters?

Metric Measuring

A decimeter is a unit used in metric measurement.

|———————————————————————|

This line is one decimeter long. A decimeter can be divided into 10 centimeters or 100 millimeters. Ten decimeters make a *meter,* which is the basic unit in the metric system. A meter is just a few inches longer than a yardstick. *Make* a *meter stick* from a long strip of cardboard or paper. Mark off the decimeters, centimeters, and millimeters.

Think in meters and surprise your friends with your new knowledge. Can you figure out the length of a football field or a 9′ x 12′ rug using the metric system?

MARCH

SAINT PATRICK'S DAY MARCH 17

Did you know that Saint Patrick, the patron saint of Ireland, wasn't even Irish at all? He was probably born in England, although Scotland and Wales claim him, too.

At the age of sixteen Patrick was captured by pirates and was held as a slave for six years. He led a life of high adventure, as well as serious study, before settling in Ireland to pursue his life's work as a bishop and Christian missionary.

The Irish loved and trusted him and still honor him today on March 17, the date of his death, over fifteen hundred years ago. When we celebrate Saint Patrick's Day, we think of shamrocks, leprechauns with shillelaghs (gnarled walking sticks), festive songs and dances, and the *wearing of the green.* In Chicago they even tint the river green!

Irish Jig

An Irish Jig will put you into the carefree spirit of the holiday!

DIRECTIONS: With hands on hips while hopping on left foot, put:

Right heel out in front, right toe across left foot;

right heel out in front and then back in place.

Now, hopping on the right foot, repeat the same pattern with the left heel out in front. If you're lucky, you can dance to a fiddle or a bagpipe!

McNamara's Band

Make your own McNamara's Band with long cardboard tube horns, coffee can drums, bells strung with yarn or elastic, juice can shakers decorated with green streamers and shamrocks . . . or attach them all to your arms and legs to make a one-man band.

Shamrock Hunt

(can be played individually or in teams)

Make several dozen three-leaf clovers from green construction paper and put a letter of the alphabet on each. (Be sure to include more vowels than consonants.) Hide them around the room along with a *few* paper four-leaf clovers without letters. On a "go" signal, players find as many clovers as they can and then put them together into *words*. The lucky four-leaf clovers can be used for any letter of the alphabet! See how many words you can spell within a time limit, using each letter only once.

Stitchery

The Irish are especially noted for their stitchery. Use a large embroidery needle and experiment with several kinds of stitches and materials to make colorful placemats, napkins, aprons, or wall hangings.

The simplest method for very young children is the Sewing Card, as described on Flag Day. Draw on a holiday design such as an Irish derby or shamrock.

On a piece of burlap or cloth sew a picture using the simple running stitch . . . try varying the colors and thicknesses of yarn or thread.

Draw a Saint Patrick's picture on a paper plate. Then sew a decorative border: punch holes along the edge of the plate and loop your yarn over the edge and through the holes. (Two paper plates stitched together and filled with beans become a tambourine!)

You can also appliqué a picture by cutting up small shapes of cloth or felt scraps and sewing them onto a larger piece of fabric.

The word "leprechaun" conjures up the imaginary world of the "wee people" of Irish legend who play their magic pipes and dance in fairy rings in enchanted gardens like this one.

Pepper Leprechaun

YOU NEED: a green pepper (or substitute an Irish potato!)

toothpicks

pieces of carrots, radishes, turnips, celery, squash, etc.

scissors

construction paper

YOU DO:
1. Using a green pepper or potato for the head or body, attach vegetable arms and legs with toothpicks.
2. Add smaller pieces for eyes, mouth, hands, ears, etc.
3. A hat, belt, and "shillelagh" cut from green construction paper will complete your Irish leprechaun.

Mulligan Stew

After Saint Patrick's Day is over, save the pepper or potato and the other vegetable "trimmings" and make a Mulligan Stew:

Cut 1½ pounds of lamb or beef into cubes. Coat with seasoned flour and brown in 3 tablespoons fat. Add some sliced onions and cover with boiling water. Simmer for 1½ hours. Add chopped potatoes, carrots, turnips, and green pepper and simmer an additional half-hour. Serve with dumplings or biscuits.

Indoor Magic Garden

YOU NEED: a large glass jar, an old fishbowl, or a terrarium
pieces of brick, clay pot, and sponge
food coloring
a mixture of
4 tablespoons ammonia, 4 tablespoons liquid bluing, and 4 tablespoons water
salt

YOU DO:
1. *Dampen* the pieces of brick, clay, and sponge and place them in a glass container.
2. *Spatter* a few drops of food coloring over the "rocks."
3. *Slowly pour* on the ammonia mixture, being careful not to splash. Then *sprinkle* salt generously over the top.

Now watch your magic garden grow! (It will take five to six hours.)

Magic Bags

This game will lead you into the make-believe world of leprechauns and can be played in pairs or by teams.

1. Give each team (or individual) a bag filled with an unrelated assortment of 3 pictures, objects, or word cards (i.e., an apple, a picture of a horse, the word "magic").
2. The teams must use the pictures or words as the *basis* for making up a story and should practice telling it before "acting it out." (Be sure to say each word at least *twice*.)
3. The audience then tries to *guess* the three key words. (Younger children might choose to show the contents of their bag before beginning, instead of making it a guessing game.)

PASSOVER

Passover (*Pesach*) is the Festival of Freedom, when Jews all over the world remember the historic exodus of the Hebrews from Egypt after four hundred and thirty years of slavery under the cruel Pharaohs.

Matzo Yeast Experiment

Matzo (unleavened bread) is an important part of the observance of Passover. The story of Passover tells us that matzo originated thousands of years ago when the Hebrews fled Egypt in such a hurry that there wasn't time to let their bread dough rise. That's why Jews still remember the event by using matzo during Passover week.

To help you understand what happened, try this experiment: Fill two glasses half full of *warm* water. Stir some flour into one glass. In the other, dissolve a little yeast in the water, then add flour. Now set them both in a warm place for an hour and watch the result!

Seder

The traditional family dinner, called the Seder, commemorates the Passover event and the approach of spring with special food, songs, and prayers. Parents and children read aloud from the Haggadah, which tells the story of the Exodus.

The youngest child asks the question "Why is this night different from all other nights?" The answers tell the meaning of each symbol on the Passover platter:

Matzo reminds us of the hardships of the long flight from Egypt when the Hebrews had to bake their bread in the hot, desert sun.

Parsley, a sign of spring and new life, is dipped into a small bowl of salt water as a remembrance of the tears of slavery.

Moror (bitter herbs) is horseradish, which also signifies the bitterness of slavery.

Haroseth represents the bricks and mortar the Hebrews used to build the Pharaoh's cities and monuments while they were slaves in Egypt.

The lamb bone recalls the paschal (sacrificial) lamb.

A roasted egg, another sign of spring, symbolizes the survival of the children of Israel.

An extra glass of wine is placed on the table and the door is opened for Elijah the prophet to come with news of freedom everywhere.

Seder Recipes

MATZO

To make matzo, mix and knead 3½ cups flour and 1 cup water. Roll out the dough on a floured surface and transfer to a greased cookie sheet. Prick all over with a fork and score into squares with a knife. Bake in a 475° preheated oven for 10 to 15 minutes or until lightly brown.

HAROSETH is easy to prepare and makes a tasty spread for your matzo. Mix 1 cup chopped apples, ¼ cup chopped nuts, 1 teaspoon cinnamon, and 2 tablespoons of grape juice or wine.

MACAROONS

Another Passover treat is macaroons made with matzo meal.

YOU NEED:
- 4 egg whites
- ¾ cup sugar
- 1½ teaspoon matzo meal
- 1 cup coconut
- 1½ teaspoon lemon juice
- 1¼ teaspoon potato starch

YOU DO: Beat egg whites and sugar and add remaining ingredients. Spoon onto a greased cookie sheet and bake until brown, about 20 minutes at 325°.

Treasure Hunt: Afikomon

The Seder dinner ends with a treasure hunt, the children's favorite. Father breaks the middle matzo (the "Afikomon," from the Greek word meaning after-meal or dessert) in half, wraps it in a napkin, and hides it; if the children find it, he must give them a "reward" to get it back. The Seder can't end until everyone has tasted a bit of the Afikomon.

APRIL

APRIL FOOLS' DAY APRIL 1

April Fools' Day originated in France in the sixteenth century when a new calendar was introduced. New Year's Day was changed from April to January, throwing everything into confusion. Because news traveled so slowly in those days, the "April Fools" were people who were still celebrating the New Year in April!

The custom of fooling friends and relatives first became popular in France, where victims were called "April fish," and later in Scotland, where they were called "April gawks." Harmless pranks are still popular today, and putting salt in the sugar bowl and pepper in the fudge are typical of the April Fools' jokes that we play on each other.

Turn-About Party

Plan a Turn-About Party for April 1. Try writing the invitations backwards while looking in the mirror. Tell everyone to wear mixed-up clothes — stripes with plaids, unmatched socks, a tie on backwards, a silly hat or shoe on the wrong foot, even a way-out hairdo. They might enjoy dressing their favorite doll or stuffed animal in crazy clothes, too!

Meet your guests at the back door, greet them with "good-bye," and remind them to walk in backwards.

Have an indoor picnic on the floor serving inside-out sandwiches with the bread in the middle, or make peanut butter pizzas. You might want to serve dessert first — an upside-down cake and punch poured from a watering can.

For a silly centerpiece use an empty flowerpot, deflated balloons, and dolls propped topsy-turvy.

Silly Games

SHOE SCRAMBLE

Everyone puts his shoes in the middle of the floor. At the "go" signal each player finds his own, puts the *left* shoe on the *right* foot, the right on the left foot, then runs back to the starting line. First one there wins!

COWS EAT BROWNIES

The leader calls out real or imaginary statements and the players respond by clapping, but *only* after a true statement. For example, Birds fly (clap, clap, clap); Leopards are spotted (clap, clap, clap); Cows eat brownies (no claps!). Keep the pace lively by chanting and clapping in rhythm. Whoever claps at the wrong time is out; last "in" is the next leader.

SILLY SENTENCES —

"Mary Makes Marvelous Muddy Mustard"

Starting with the youngest member of the group, who says her name, every player, in turn, adds a word to make up a silly sentence. Each word must begin with the first letter of that name. Use four to six words for each silly sentence and continue playing until everyone's name has been tried. Example: *Billy Bounces Billions of Beans in the Bathtub.*

This game can also be played by passing around a sheet of paper for each person to *write* a word. The last player then reads the silly sentence aloud.

The same method can be used to draw crazy characters, by adding parts of the body instead of words. This version is more fun if you fold the paper to hide your drawing before passing it on to the next player.

APRIL FOOLERS

YOU NEED: newspapers or magazines
               scissors
               glue or paste
               construction paper
               crayons or markers

YOU DO:
1. Cut out several pictures from newspapers or magazines, or draw your own.
2. Paste each picture on a piece of construction paper, *omitting*, *adding*, or *changing* one part to make it look foolish (a school bus with the lettering backwards, flowers growing upside down, a bicycle with a wheel missing).
3. Take turns guessing what's wrong with each silly picture. Can you fool your friends?

Another Fooler: You might also *combine* pictures that don't go together (a mailman wearing a stethoscope, a football player holding a bat, a beard on a baby, or a pumpkin on a Christmas tree). Who can think up the silliest combinations?

WACKY ART CONTEST

Each player is given a slip of paper with the name of an object written on it (a pig, a pair of glasses, a shoe, a candlestick, etc.). He must then draw a picture of the item with his left hand (or right hand if he is left-handed) and everyone tries to guess what he has drawn. See how many correct guesses each picture gets.

Variation. Give silly assignments like a cross-eyed pig, a 3-pouched kangaroo or a double-ended spoon.

EASTER

Easter is the most important holy day of the Christian religion. The rising sun is the symbol of Easter and the Resurrection of Jesus Christ.

The date of Easter is not always the same because it is related to the full moon and the position of the sun over the equator. The earliest possible date is March 22, the latest, April 25.

The Easter egg symbolizes birth and a "new beginning." Long ago some people even believed that the earth had hatched from a giant egg! The tradition of coloring and exchanging eggs was started by the ancient Egyptians. There are many ways that you can join in the fun of coloring and decorating your own Easter eggs.

Coloring the Eggs

DYEING EGGS

The easiest way to color eggs (either hard-boiled or blown) is to dye them with commercial food coloring (liquid or tablets). Be sure to add 1 tablespoon of vinegar to each cup of dye. Try making new colors by mixing red, yellow, and blue in various combinations.

Tips:
* To hard-boil eggs without cracking them, cover eggs (at room temperature) with water and bring to a full boil. Remove from heat, replace lid, and let stand 25 minutes. Rinse in cold water.
* To make blown eggs, use a darning needle or thin nail; poke a small hole in one end of the egg and a larger hole in the other. Blow through the small hole to empty the eggshell. (Refrigerate contents for later use in cooking.) Rinse out the shell carefully, then air-dry it.

When working on your eggs, the egg carton makes a handy rack!

You may want to experiment with other more "eggs-otic" ways of dyeing eggs.

CRAYON RESIST
Use a light-colored crayon to draw on a name or design, then dip the egg in dye and the ink or wax will show through.

CHECKED, STRIPED, PLAID
Put rubber bands or narrow masking tape around the egg, then dip into dye. After the egg has dried completely, remove the rubber bands or tape.

TIE-DYE
Wrap the egg in a 5" x 6" piece of cloth and fasten with a rubber band at each end. Soak the wrapped egg in dye (1 cup solution for every 2 eggs), remove it, and leave it in the cloth to dry overnight. Unwrap and presto! you have a beautiful tie-dyed egg.

BATIK
Hold a lighted birthday candle over the egg and drip some wax on it. (This will become the white part of your design.) Now dip the egg into some dye until it turns the shade you want. Add more wax if you wish, and dip into a second color. You may leave the wax on, or soften it in a barely warm oven, before rubbing it off with a cloth.

LEAF PRINTS
Make patterns on your eggs by wrapping them with leaves and ferns before dyeing, as people did long ago.

NATURAL DYES

You may want to be adventuresome and make your own dyes using natural materials as country people have done through the ages. These produce very soft shades of color that can't be obtained from commercial dyes.

YOU NEED: for yellow: saffron, crocuses, daffodils, or yellow onionskins

for green: young grass, broccoli, spinach, escarole, moss, rhubarb, or birch leaves

for blue: blueberries

for brown: plums, coffee, tea, or walnut shells

YOU DO:
1. *Wash and chop* up the raw material, place in a pot (enamel is best) and cover with water.
2. *Boil* for at least 5 minutes (longer to make colors darker).
3. *Strain* through a colander lined with cheesecloth or a clean rag.
4. *Cool,* then gently dip your hard-boiled or blown-out eggs into the solution for several minutes.

However you choose to dye your eggs, you can make them shine with a few drops of vegetable oil on a soft cloth.

PAINTING EGGS

Although the quickest and most popular method of coloring eggs is with dye, you might want to follow an Eastern European custom of painting them with special symbols to wish friends well at Eastertime.

sun — *good luck*
deer — *good health*
hen and rooster — *wishes come true*
flowers — *love and beauty*

To paint your Easter eggs, use a small brush and watercolors or tempera. Apply varnish if you want a shiny finish.

Decorating Eggs

You don't need to dye eggs to make them beautiful! Just add some decorations.

Young children will have more success with hard-boiled eggs using these simple materials.

* Collage — Glue on stars, seals, canceled stamps, or looseleaf reinforcement rings.
* Yarn — Draw on a simple design with liquid glue; let it dry partially, then add on yarn.
* Comic strips — Glue on favorite cartoon characters. Smooth out wrinkles and let dry. Shellac, if desired.

Older children may prefer to use blown eggs, which can be kept and enjoyed from year to year. Although the following methods take more time, the results are worth the effort. Just glue on some of these items:

* Tiny flowers cut from seed catalogues, wallpaper, or wrapping paper.
* Animals and designs cut from cloth (dampen cloth slightly before gluing).
* Pasta, seed, beans. Glue items on half of the egg at a time. Let dry; then turn and finish the other half. Spray-paint it, if desired.
* Binsegrass (Polish yarn eggs). Apply glue to both ends of a blown egg and wrap yarn around the glued areas. Fill in the middle section with your own designs.

Also, try etched eggs. With a needle or knife, scratch a design onto eggs that have been dyed in deep, vivid colors.

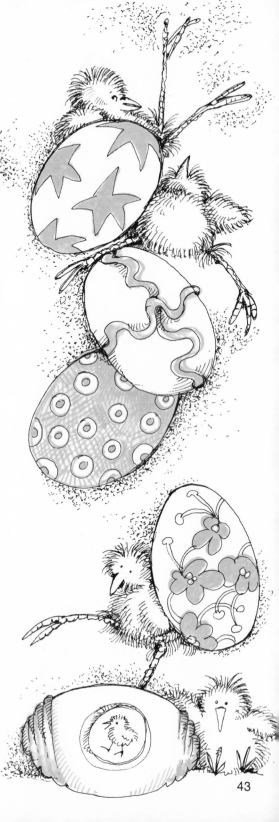

Other Easter Decorations

According to a Hindu myth, the giaint egg that was once the world broke in two. One half turned gold and became the sky, the other turned silver and became the earth. The mountains, rivers, and clouds came from layers under the shell.

SHADOW-BOX EGGS

Create your own miniature world inside an egg. The simpler way is to hinge together two egg carton sections with tape. Paint and then fill with spring flowers, chicks, and bunnies made from paper, gumdrops, and marshmallows.

Older children could try a more delicate project by using the blown egg itself.

1. Dye the egg.
2. Cut out a window with manicure scissors (poke a small hole to start).
3. Brush several coats of clear nail polish on the inside of the shell to strengthen it.
4. Add a dab of clay (covered with Easter grass) in the bottom of the egg and stick in some tiny flowers or miniature figures.
5. Glue some thin braid, yarn, or rickrack around the cut edge to reinforce it.
6. Coat the outside with several layers of clear lacquer or nail polish.

EGG CRADLE

Use two plastic egg halves, one (resting vertically) for the canopy and the other set inside it (horizontally) for the bed. Anchor them together with glue or a dab of clay. Make a "baby" by painting a face on a small cork, button or bead and "tuck it in" with a tiny piece of cloth or tissue.

STAND-UP ANIMALS AND PEOPLE: ideal placecards or table favors made from hard-boiled eggs.

Just glue these *trimmings* to the egg face or body:

Hair. cotton, yarn, paper, or pot scrubbers.

Facial features. bits of cloth or paper, sequins (or draw them on with paint or felt markers).

Ears, tails, whiskers. pipe cleaners, felt scraps, yarn, or straws.

To make stands for your egg figures, glue on curtain rings, corks, small bottle caps or a cardboard tube cut into circles *or* roll and glue small strips of cardboard into cylinders for a collar or legs.

EGG DISPLAYS

To display your blown-out egg originals, hang them on a mobile or from a tree. To make the stand and tree, first fill a coffee can with plaster of Paris and, when partially hard, insert a sturdy branch. Spray-paint the branch and cover the can, if you wish; add some Easter grass and decorate.

Hint for hanging: First glue a tiny piece of macaroni or small bead on the egg and then loop a thread through it.

EASTER BASKETS

Instead of buying a basket, be original and make your own. Use a sand pail or tomato basket, or add a rope or ribbon handle to a large oatmeal or milk carton or cut-off plastic bleach bottle. Paint or cover your container with crepe or contact paper and decorate with flowers, bunnies, and other Easter cutouts.

EASTER BONNETS

Design a "fashionable" hat for the neighborhood parade complete with ribbons, lace, and flowers — who would believe it's all made of paper! A cardboard or Styrofoam food tray, box lid, egg carton, paper plate, or berry basket makes an ideal base. Add Easter grass and then glue on festive cutouts, as above. Popsicle sticks, pipe cleaners, or cardboard tubes will make your decorations stand up.

Egg Recipes

It's always a lot more fun to dye Easter eggs than to eat them!
So here are some recipes for those endless leftovers.

Try these ideas with the uncooked eggs you've been saving.

There is a saying that "the sun dances for joy on Easter at dawn and those who see it will have good luck all year," so why not try:

SUNRISE SANDWICHES

YOU NEED: 4 whole, unsliced hamburger buns
4 eggs
margarine or soft butter
4 slices cheese
salt and pepper

YOU DO:
1. Preheat oven to 325°.
2. Cut a hole in center of each bun (1 inch deep but not through the bottom) with a biscuit or cookie cutter.
3. Carefully lift out the circle with a fork and butter the inside of the opening.
4. Place the buns on a cookie sheet and drop an egg into each hole. Sprinkle with salt and pepper.
5. Bake 25 minutes. Then top with cheese slices (or grated cheese). Bake 5 minutes more. Serve immediately.

EGGS IN A NEST

Mix 2 cups mashed potatoes with ½ cup chopped ham or bacon bits, 3 tablespoons chopped parsley, salt, and paprika. Spread the mixture in a greased baking dish. Make 4 hollows in the potatoes and spoon in 4 eggs. Sprinkle with bread crumbs and dot with butter. Bake at 325° for 12 minutes (until eggs are firm, not hard).

Of course, don't forget such easy favorites as French Toast and Omelets.

TUNA BURGERS

Mix chopped hard-boiled eggs with tuna, diced celery and onion, pickle relish, and mayonnaise. Spread on lightly toasted English muffins; cover with a slice of cheese and broil a minute or two until the cheese melts.

You can also use your hard-boiled eggs in seafood, potato, or egg salad — the obvious — or hide them in a meatloaf! Deviled eggs (yolks mashed with mayonnaise, a little dry mustard and repacked into the white halves) are fun to make and eat.

Especially for the toddler . . .

Two Bunny Rhymes

(use body and facial motions to act them out)

Here is a bunny *(make a fist)*
With ears so funny *(wiggle two fingers)*
And here is a hole in the ground *(make a hole with other hand)*

When a noise he hears
He pricks up his ears *(extend fingers fully)*
And jumps in the hole in the ground!

Here comes a bunny
Hip-hop-hop
See how his long ears
Flip-flop-flop

See how his nose goes
Twink-twink-twink
See how his eyes go
Wink-wink-wink

Easter Games

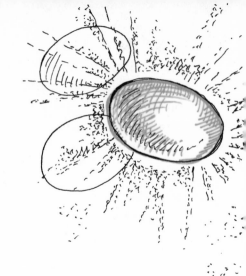

Give a new twist to your Easter Egg Hunt!

EGG HUNT I
1. Hide paper or dyed eggs of various colors.
2. Give each color a value: 5 for blue, 4 for yellow, 3 for red, 2 for green, etc.; a silver foil egg could be worth the most. (You can mark the numbers right on the eggs.)
3. The one who gets the highest score is the winner.

BUNNY HUNT — *Hide the "bunny" and hand out the eggs*

YOU NEED: construction paper
crayon or felt marker
scissors
a treasure for each player: small chocolate bunnies, candy eggs, or kisses

YOU DO:
1. Write several clues on pieces of paper cut in the shape of eggs. Number each one. (Picture clues could be made for younger children.)
2. Hide all the clues *in order* except #1 (#2 could be hidden under the radio, #3 under Dad's pillow, etc.), so the children will always know where to look *next*.
3. Explain the rules and then give the children clue #1 to start the hunt. Let them follow the hints until the last clue leads them to the hidden "bunny" (chocolate, marshmallow, or the like), or another surprise.

EGG HUNT II

Fill egg carton "eggs" (two sections taped together) with surprises, such as candy, pennies, paper clips, small stones, beans, Easter grass, rice, buttons, etc. See who finds the heaviest, lightest, noisiest, sweetest, etc., item. Guess what's inside.

Variation. Matching Eggs. Fill and hide pairs of eggs with identical objects and have children try to match the eggs. Trades can be made. Who has the most pairs?

It's traditional to play *games* with the colorful eggs found on the hunt. The most famous of these has been played on Easter Monday since 1878, when President Rutherford B. Hayes invited children to the White House lawn.

WHITE HOUSE EGG ROLL

Give each player an Easter egg. He must then push it with his nose around a set course on the floor or grass

or

Roll the eggs to the bottom of a slope without breaking them.

EGG RUNNING CONTEST

Set up teams in relay fashion; each player in turn runs with an egg balanced on a spoon!

ANOTHER "OLD-TIMER"

Roll or push the eggs toward a shallow hole. A large tin can or a milk carton turned on its side can also be used as a target.

49

MAY

MAY DAY MAY 1

For centuries May Day has signaled the arrival of spring greenery after the cold, dreary winter. Singing, dancing, and flowers everywhere have always been a part of this joyful celebration. Like so many festivals, May Day dates back to the ancient Romans, who brought offerings to the temple of Flora, the goddess of springtime. The first child to place a garland on the altar of the temple would have good luck the whole year long.

Welcome spring! Gather some fresh *flowers,* or create beautiful homemade ones from construction, crepe, or tissue paper, foil . . . and even egg cartons.

Paper Flowers

SIMPLE FLOWERS

Draw and cut out basic flower shapes from tissue, construction, or crepe paper. Flute or curl the edges.

EGG CARTON TULIPS OR DAFFODILS

Scallop the edges of individual egg carton cups and paint in bright spring colors.

POM-POMS

Fringe a long strip of crepe paper, bunch together, and wind tape or wire around the bottom.

ROSES AND CARNATIONS

To make individual petals, trace and cut out tissue or crepe paper circles. Fold each circle into fourths; scallop the edge for a rose or zig-zag for a carnation. Open the circle; then twist at the base and secure with tape or thread. For a fuller flower, combine several layers.

SILVER DAISY

Cut a piece of foil approximately 7" x 6" and fold it lengthwise. Cut a row of petals along the open side, stopping about ½ inch from the folded base. Wrap the daisy petals around a paper center, pinching the foil together at the bottom.

Whatever flower you create, use wire, pipe cleaners, straws, or Popsicle sticks covered with crepe paper for stems and add paper leaves. To make a contrasting center for any of the flowers, cover a bean or piece of wadded paper with a scrap of crepe paper; twist the ends leaving enough to attach the petals and stems.

Flower Arrangements

DRIED FLOWERS

Choose brightly colored fresh flowers to preserve.
Mix 1 cup Borax and 2 cups cornmeal together and pour half of the mixture into a shoebox. Leave 1-inch stems on the flowers and lay them face down in the box. Cover with the remaining mixture and leave at room temperature with the lid on for 3 to 4 weeks.

OLD-FASHIONED NOSEGAYS

Surround dried, fresh, or paper flowers with a lace doily and tie with a pretty ribbon.

MINIATURE BOUQUETS

Place your flowers in a decorated container — a small juice can, a cardboard tissue tube, a paper cup, or a spray can lid. (Add a dab of clay, if needed.) For a springy touch, attach beads or little paper birds, butterflies, or bumblebees to pipe cleaner stems . . . or arrange a few tiny flowers in an empty painted spool tied with a ribbon.

MAY BASKET

Surprise someone special by hanging a colorful *May Basket* on his door.

Decorate a *berry basket* by weaving strips of construction paper, ribbon, or yarn in and out of the openings. Add a paper, ribbon, or yarn handle; braid for an old-fashioned look.

Make a *parasol basket* using a paper cone as a base. A lace doily will give a frilly look.

You might also make a May Basket by folding a square of construction paper four times and cutting slits in four places as shown. Glue the ends together and add a handle.

Long ago in England where May Day was the merriest holiday of all, the most important tradition was bringing home the May tree. Early in the morning the villagers hunted through the forest for the largest tree they could find. Often it took many teams of oxen just to carry it to town! Soon it was set up on the village green and gaily decorated for the dancing and the crowning of the May Queen.

Maypole

Have you ever danced around a *Maypole*? Decorate a pole or tree with crepe paper, ribbons, and flowers. Hang long cloth or crepe paper streamers from the top.

Maypole Dance

Everyone forms a circle around the pole with each dancer holding one of the streamers.

Skip to the right 16 steps; skip to the left 16 steps; skip to the center (hands raised high); skip back to place.

Try some variations: Form two circles and skip in opposite directions. One person at a time weaves in and out of the circle and back again. Partners face each other and make a chain, dancing "a grand right and left."

What other patterns can you weave with the streamers?

Wind and Flowers

A May Day Game

Players divide into two teams, the Flowers and the Wind. They stand facing each other behind two boundary lines placed far apart. The Flowers choose a secret name (Marigolds, Petunias) and hop or dance close to the Wind's baseline. The Wind players call out names of flowers and when someone guesses the secret one, the Flowers *turn* and *rush* back to their line, trying not to get caught by the Wind. The tagged players join the Wind and the game continues with a new flower name for each round. When all the Flowers are caught, the two original teams can change places and play again.

JUNE

FLAG DAY JUNE 14

Did you know that when George Washington asked Betsy Ross to sew the very first American flag in 1777, it had just thirteen five-pointed stars all in a circle? That was the year when on June 14 the Continental Congress proclaimed that the design of the flag should be thirteen red and white stripes (standing for the thirteen original colonies) with the stars set in a field of blue.

Our flag is more than just a cloth banner; it is a symbol of our country and the courage, purity, and justice that the red, white, and blue represent. Since 1916 all of the states observe Flag Day by flying "Old Glory" from federal buildings.

Flag Picture

Draw a picture of our flag as it looks today. Be sure to include seven red and six white stripes, as well as all fifty stars, one for each state. Can you find out when the last two stars (for Alaska and Hawaii) were added?

A Flag Sewing Card

YOU NEED: a piece of cardboard or a food tray from the grocery store
red, white, and blue yarn
masking tape
crayons
scissors
a knitting needle or a paper punch

YOU DO:
1. Draw the flag on your cardboard; then punch holes around the star area and at each end of the stripes. Color in or add gummed stars. (For an easier sewing card make a large 5-pointed star with a hole at each tip.)
2. To help in threading, wrap masking tape around one end of the yarn before pulling it through the holes.

Why not make a sewing card of flags from other countries?

MOTHER'S AND FATHER'S DAYS

Father's Day preceded Mother's Day by four years. It was inspired by Mrs. John Bruce Dold, who along with her brothers and sisters, was raised by her father after her mother's death. It was first celebrated on June 19, 1910.

The observance of Mother's Day is the result of the tireless efforts of Miss Anna Jarvis of Philadelphia. Her desire to honor her own mother (of eleven children) and all mothers was fulfilled in 1914, when President Wilson made the second Sunday in May the official day. A much older tradition in England is "Mothering Sunday," observed during Lent, while in many other parts of Europe Saint Anne's Day has long been a special occasion for mothers.

Make these days more special for your Mom, Dad, or your grandparents by creating a personal gift for them to enjoy for many years.

Hands Down

YOU NEED: a shallow pan
tempera paint
newspapers
several sheets of paper
a felt marker or crayons

YOU DO:

1. Cover the bottom of the pan with a small amount of tempera paint. (Spread newspapers where you are working.)
2. Place your hand into the paint and then press it firmly down on a piece of paper. Make several prints and choose the one you like best. (Keep a pail of water handy to wash off the paint.)
3. After everyone has chosen his favorite, paste them on one large sheet of paper. Write your name and age next to your own print. Across the top add a message to Mom or Dad . . . and be sure to include the date!

I Remember Mama (or Papa) — A Memory Collage

YOU NEED: a picture frame and cardboard to fit it
old magazines, newspapers, and photographs
scissors
glue

YOU DO:

1. Make or buy a picture frame and cut a piece of cardboard to fit.
2. Collect items that remind you of Mom or Dad, such as a shopping list, a letter, a telephone "doodle," a vacation memento, a pressed flower, or a ticket stub from a movie or ballgame.
3. Cut out pictures, words, and numbers from newspapers and magazines showing their favorite foods, sports, songs, TV shows, hobbies, books, and important dates.
4. Ask Grandma for some photos of Mom or Dad as a child and include some recent ones, too.
5. Arrange all of the collected items on the cardboard in an interesting, *overlapping* design. Then glue each piece in place. (These same items could be assembled and glued into a scrapbook.)

Silhouettes

YOU NEED: 2 sheets of construction paper (contrasting colors)
pencil
tape
light (lamp or flashlight)

YOU DO:
1. Tape a piece of paper on the refrigerator or wall.
2. Take turns sitting in front of the paper (try not to wiggle!).
3. Use a bright lamp (remove shade if necessary) or flashlight to cast a shadow of each child's profile on the paper.
4. Have an adult or older child lightly trace the outline with a pencil; then cut out the silhouette, turn it over and glue it onto a contrasting background.
5. Cover your picture with clear contact paper or frame it, if you wish. Mount each picture individually or group them together in a family portrait.

Pancakes for Papa

Greet Dad (or Mom) with a special breakfast ...

YOU NEED:
pancake mix (with necessary added ingredients)
spoon
mixing bowl
frying pan or griddle
cooking oil
butter
syrup
fruit

YOU DO:
1. Make the pancakes according to the directions on the box. Add thin slices of bananas, apples, peaches, strawberries, or a few blueberries — whichever is Dad or Mom's favorite — to the batter.
2. Surprise Dad with an extra pancake in the shape of an animal! Pour the base, then *quickly* add head, ears, tail. Flip over carefully.
3. Arrange a tray with a placemat, napkin, and silverware. Don't forget a glass of juice, a hot cup of coffee, a spring flower, and a homemade card, just for Mom or Dad.

My Father Likes . . .

YOU NEED: paper
                     yarn
                     magazines and newspapers
                     scissors
                     glue
                     crayons or felt markers

YOU DO:

1. Put several sheets of paper together into a book; punch two holes and tie with yarn.
2. Draw or paste a picture of Dad on the front with the title "My Father Likes . . ."
3. Hunt through magazines and newspapers for pictures that show what Dad enjoys (a person fishing, gardening, jogging, or playing the piano; a pipe, a camera, a hot fudge sundae).
4. Put one picture on each page along with the first letter of the *word* that it depicts.
5. On Father's Day ask Dad to look at the pictures with you and fill in the missing letters.

Of course, this could be a book, "My Mom Likes . . ." too.

Growing Stick

YOU NEED: a board approximately 2″ x 4″ x 6′ or strips of cardboard or brown paper
sandpaper
paint
a felt marker
felt
rickrack
trim (optional)

YOU DO:

1. Use a board (sand the rough edges) or tape 6 feet of cardboard together. (You could also draw a ruler right on the inside of a closet door.)
2. With a yardstick as a guide, mark off the feet and inches.
3. Decorate with paint, felt, rickrack, or other trim.
4. Prop or tape the "giant ruler" against a wall. Then have each member of the family stand against it and mark his height, initials, and date. Don't forget to continue to record your family's growth from time to time!

Put on a Play

For Mother's or Father's Day...you play the parents and let them be the kids! It's great fun to "reverse the roles" and discover how we see each other. Think up everyday situations to act out: a typical breakfast table conversation, bedtime, a car trip, choosing a TV show, grocery shopping, a family picnic...

A Poetic Touch

What could be more meaningful than a poem you've written yourself to tell Mom and Dad how you feel about them?

Have you ever tried to write a poem? Here are several ways to spark your imagination and help you get started.

1. Think about what Mom and Dad mean to you and what makes them special.
2. Make a list of the things you like to do together.
3. Get into a poetic mood by listening to music, reading a book of poetry or a favorite story, or leafing through a family album.

Remember, you don't have to rhyme your words...the important thing is to be yourself and express your thoughts freely. (Younger children could dictate their poems to an older brother or sister.)

MAKE A POETRY BOOK

For a gift for any occasion, collect poems that you particularly enjoy, including some of your own, and illustrate them.

JULY

INDEPENDENCE DAY
THE FOURTH OF JULY

It was two o'clock in the afternoon on July 4, 1776. In Philadelphia people had been gathering around the courthouse since dawn in anticipation of the momentous event. Suddenly the Liberty Bell rang out the news that the Declaration of Independence had been signed. This important document proclaimed, in the words of Thomas Jefferson (its chief author), "... these united colonies are, and of right ought to be, free and independent states...."

John Adams, who like Jefferson would later become one of our presidents, wrote a letter to his wife suggesting that the day should be celebrated with prayers, but also with "... pomp and parade, with shows, games, sports, guns, bells, bonfires, and illuminations, from one end of this continent to the other ..."

Parade

Wave your flags and Join the PARADE to celebrate the birthday of our country! Carry a small paper pennant taped to a Popsicle stick ... or stretch a large banner between two cardboard hanger tubes.

Tie several wagons together to make a "wagon train" (you might even build a float on one) or get in line on your scooter or skateboard. Ride your bicycle or tricycle weaving red, white, and blue "bunting" in and out of the spokes; add paper streamers or small flags to the handlebars.

Be a Yankee Doodle Dandy! Ride your own *hobby horse* in the parade. Use an old broomstick, a yardstick, a long wrapping paper tube, or rolled newspapers for the body. A stuffed paper bag or two pieces of felt sewn together could serve as the head. Add ears, a mane, etc. "Stick a feather in your cap and call it macaroni!"

Wear the *uniform* of the American Revolution — a jacket, knickers, and stockings, plus a tricornered hat on your head and foil-covered cardboard buckles on your shoes. A few patriots playing their coffee can "drums" and cardboard tube "fifes" will complete the parade ... or almost ... don't forget your pets. Decorate their leashes, collars, cages, and bowls and bring them along!

4th PARADE

Carnival

Have a Fourth of July CARNIVAL featuring booths and games with an Independence Day theme.

SIGN IN, PLEASE

Tack a copy of the Declaration of Independence on a tree. Have everyone sign his own "John Hancock" on a small square of paper with Thomas Jefferson's pen (tie or tape a feather on it). These signatures can be first taped to the Declaration and later drawn out of "Uncle Sam's hat" (a decorated oatmeal or ice cream carton) for a prize.

HAPPY BIRTHDAY RING TOSS

Make a "cake" target from a hatbox or a large ice cream or carry-out chicken carton. For a candle, poke a hole in the center and push through a long cardboard tube (towel or coat hanger) and secure with tape. "Frost" with red, white, and blue paint or crepe paper and add a paper flame to the candle. For the rings, you can use plastic six-pack or cardboard circles.

UNCLE SAM'S FISH POND

First make a fishing pole with a stick, string, and magnet. Write fortunes on paper or cardboard fish and attach a paperclip to each. Mark "U.S." for Uncle Sam on a few. Everyone tries to catch a fish; the player who snags one stamped "U.S." wins a prize.

BIRTHDAY CANDLE SQUIRT

Aim your water gun at a lighted candle and try to put out the flame. (An adult or older child should be on hand to light the candles.)

STATES SHUFFLEBOARD

Get a map of your state from a service station or make your own. Draw large circles around the capital and other cities and landmarks, assigning a point value to each. Be sure to include your own hometown. Tape the map to a driveway or sidewalk. Aim for the circles by pushing red, white, and blue poker chips or jar lids with a broom or hockey stick.

LIBERTY BELL BEANBAG TOSS

Hang a bell from a tree branch. Try to ring the bell by tossing beanbags or tennis balls.

COLONIAL ROULETTE

Draw 13 squares on a piece of shelf paper and write the name of one of the 13 original colonies on each one, numbering them from 1 to 13: Massachusetts, Connecticut, Rhode Island, Virginia, Georgia, North Carolina, South Carolina, New York, Pennsylvania, New Jersey, Delaware, Maryland, and New Hampshire. Make a "roulette wheel" out of heavy cardboard (a pizza tray is ideal); divide it into 13 numbered sections and attach it to a tree or post. Have each player place his marker on a colony before spinning. Markers could be poker chips, pennies, cardboard disks, or birthday candles.

Refreshment Booth

Set up a cold drink and bakery stand. Keep the lemonade or fruit punch chilled to satisfy your thirsty Fourth of July customers. Don't forget a cash box because *everyone* will stop by this booth!

PAINTBRUSH COOKIES

"Paint" these to sell in the booth. Use your favorite sugar cookie recipe or use this one:

1. *Mix:* ⅓ cup soft shortening
   ⅓ cup sugar
   ⅔ cup honey
   1 egg
   1 teaspoon vanilla
2. *Stir in:* 2 ¾ cups sifted flour
   1 teaspoon salt.
   1 teaspoon baking soda
3. *Chill.*
4. *Roll out and cut* into Fourth of July shapes: a flag, a firecracker, a candle, Uncle Sam's Hat.
5. Put on a *greased* cookie sheet and bake 8 to 10 minutes at 375°.
6. When cool, paint on designs with "Egg Yolk Paint": For each color blend 1 egg yolk with ¼ teaspoon water and food coloring and pour mixture into a muffin tin. Use small brushes to paint on your holiday designs. (Add a few drops of water if mixture gets thick.)

NO-BAKE PATRIOTIC COOKIES

1. Melt and stir ¼ cup margarine with 3 cups miniature marshmallows.
2. Remove from heat and divide mixture equally into three bowls.
3. Add a few drops of red food coloring to one bowl and blue to the second, leaving the third one plain.
4. Stir 1⅓ cups of dried cereal into each bowl.

Hints: Grease your hands before shaping the cookies and work quickly while the batter is still warm. Let cool on waxed paper.

MOON DAY JULY 20

On July 20, 1969, an American astronaut named Neil Armstrong landed on the moon! When he stepped out of his Apollo spacecraft, "The Eagle," and put his foot down on the moon's powdery surface, he said these now-famous words: "One small step for man, one giant leap for mankind."

Can you remember the names of the two other astronauts who went on this famous space mission? (Answer: Edwin Aldrin, Charles Conrad, Jr.)

Be an Astronaut

Fashion a *spacesuit* from a large box by cutting armholes and a head opening, leaving the bottom open for your legs. Use a smaller box or grocery bag for your space helmet. You might add pipe cleaner antennae, and earphones made from two paper cups connected by string.

Create a *spaceship* or *rocket* from a large packing box. Be sure to include a control panel with buttons and switches and a telephone for talking to Earth. Make an oxygen tank out of a potato chip can and attach it to the helmet with a piece of rubber hose or a stuffed nylon stocking or long sock.

Plaster-Cast Footprints

Make a cast of your footprints.

YOU NEED:
plaster of Paris and water or soft clay
a paper plate, pie tin, or a box lid
soapsuds or Vaseline

YOU DO:
1. Mix the plaster of Paris according to directions on the package.
2. Pour a thin layer (about 2 inches) into a shallow container.
3. After coating your foot with Vaseline or soapsuds, step into the plaster; press down firmly and step *quickly* out again. (Have a bucket of water handy to wash your foot.)

Moonscape

Glue small objects — coins, pieces of macaroni or straws, buttons, nuts, and bolts — onto the outside of a bowl, margarine tub, paper plate, box, or the like. Cover with heavy-duty foil, pinching in around each object; then dab on black ink or paint with a rag or sponge to make it look like the moon's shadowy surface.

Moon Experiment

Who would believe, when looking up at the bright moonlight, that the moon is really dark? If it weren't for the light of the sun, you wouldn't see the moon at all! What you see are the sun's rays reflecting (or bouncing off) the lunar surface as the moon travels around the earth each month.

Try this experiment:

YOU NEED: a white ball attached to a piece of string (Styrofoam, tennis, Ping-Pong)
a light (a table lamp without a shade)

YOU DO:
1. Pretending that the ball is the moon, the lamp is the sun, and you are watching from the earth, stand facing the lamp in a dark room, holding the ball by the string in front of you.
2. Next, slowly move the ball to your left. Can you see a sliver of light that looks like a crescent moon?
3. Continue to move the ball (as *you* gradually turn left, too). Soon half of the ball will be lighted by the "sun." When will you see a "full moon"?

What happens to the lighted side of the "moon" as you turn completely around? Do you now see why the moon *appears* to change shape?

Moon Games

MOON JUMP
Draw a 6-foot line with chalk on the floor or sidewalk. This shows the length of a single step that a spaceman makes on the moon. Starting at one end, see how many jumps it takes you on earth to equal one moon step!

MOON TAG
Players must slowly bounce from place to place with arms extended, as if floating weightlessly in space.

MOON HOPSCOTCH
Draw a hopscotch course with a "spaceship" square at the start and the moon at the finish. Each player has his own "moonrock" for tossing.

MOON MAN, MAY I?
Line up and move *one at a time* toward the finish line by following the directions from the Moon Man. Moon Man: "Sally, you may take two crater hops," or "George, you may take one leap," or "Tom, take three blastoffs." After each command, the Spacewalker must say, "Moon Man, may I?" in order to move. If he forgets, he must go back to the beginning. The leader continues to give directions, some for steps forward, some backward, until the first Spacewalker touches the finish line (crater) and becomes the next Moon Man.

MOON RELAY
The players (astronauts) form two teams; each team is given three sheets of paper (moon rocks). At a signal the first astronaut in each line lays down the sheets, one in front of the other, and steps from rock to rock, each time picking up the back sheet and moving it to the front. When he reaches the finish line, he picks up all three sheets and races back to hand them to the next player in line.

AUGUST

A NO-HOLIDAY MONTH!

You may just want to relax and play and enjoy the long, hot summer days . . . or you could think up your own way to celebrate these unheralded August events:

August 2 — The first Lincoln penny was issued (1909).

August 3 — Columbus set sail for the "New Land" (1492).

August 12 — Thomas Edison invented the phonograph (1877).

August 17 — Davy Crockett was born (1786).

August 19 — National Aviation Day celebrates the birthday of Orville Wright, who with his brother Wilbur, flew the first airplane. (1903).

August 26 — Women's Rights Day (1920). Women were finally permitted to vote.

If you're really lucky, your birthday comes in August so you won't have to look for something special to celebrate!

SEPTEMBER

LABOR DAY

Labor Day honors working people by giving them time off for rest and relaxation. Since it comes near the end of summer, just before the school bell rings, it's an ideal time for a family picnic . . . in the park or your own backyard.

Indian-Style Pit Fire

Pack a picnic basket, or cookout over an *Indian-Style Pit Fire.* Dig a shallow hole and encircle it with rocks or bricks. In the center build a "tepee" of dry twigs and surround it with larger sticks, "log cabin" fashion. When the kindling catches fire, add still larger sticks and branches to keep it going. Place a grate across the rocks.

Campfire Stew

A favorite cookout dinner (in addition to the 57 varieties of hot dogs and hamburgers!) is *Campfire Stew*: Just brown onions and ground meat in a pot or skillet and add your favorite hearty soups, water, and catsup. Cover, let simmer, and then spoon piping hot into bowls. Serve with cornbread, which can be baked covered by putting two foil pans together.

Outdoor Games

After supper is over, play **LABOR DAY CHARADES**, pantomiming various occupations, or set up some active outdoor games using leftover paper supplies. (Don't forget to put out your fire and clean up before you leave!)

PAPER PLATE DISCUS THROW

Draw a starting line and see who can toss his plate the farthest, the highest, etc.

CUP TOSS

Line up several paper cups. Number each one and see who can score the most points by tossing in bottle caps or stones.

ROPE AND CLOTHESPIN GAMES AND RELAYS

A rope and some clothespins tucked away in your picnic basket will spark ideas for many games, such as tug-of-war or jump-rope or relay races.

For a *shuttle relay*, each team passes a clothespin down the row and back again; over heads, through legs, etc.

A *rope relay* is played like this: String the rope between two trees; then divide the group into teams, giving the first person on each team four clothespins. He must run to the line and attach the pins, then return to tag the second player, who removes the pins and gives them to the third player, etc. The first team to finish is the winner!

Don't forget the old favorite, *Drop the Clothespin*. Use any container that you have handy, and try to drop the clothespins in one by one.

TAG GAMES

Who wants to be It for a tag game?

Chinese tag. Player who is tagged must *hold* the tagged *spot* on his body with one hand until he can tag another person.

Chain tag. Tagged persons "link elbows" with the leader. *Chain* grows until all are caught.

Safety zone. No one can be tagged who is touching a *tree* or *stone* (only one player to a safety zone).

Shadow. Play this game at night near a porch light. Try to *step on* someone's shadow . . . or using a flashlight, try to catch someone with the beam.

For the next two games, players form a large circle with the leader in the center:

Number tag. Each player is given a number. The leader then calls out two numbers and players called try to exchange places before the leader can tag one and take *his* place (and number).

Stoop tag. Everyone skips around and sings a song. *When the song ends,* players must all try to stoop down before being tagged.

MORE RELAYS TO TRY
On-and-Off Sweater Relay
  (use an oversized sweater)
Book on Head
Potato or Corncob on a Spoon
Hopping Inside a Sack
"Skating" on Paper Plates
Hopping with a Cup of Water

American Indian Day was proclaimed a holiday in 1916 by President Woodrow Wilson "to recognize, honor and better the conditions of the American Indian." It is celebrated in many states on the fourth Friday in September.

AMERICAN INDIAN DAY

The native Americans, through their beautiful weaving, pottery, leatherwork, and jewelry, have contributed greatly to the artistic heritage of America. Today, all Americans are interested in preserving these authentic crafts and reviving other traditions of Indian life.

Arts and Crafts Exhibit

Plan an Indian Exhibition in your school or neighborhood. First collect pictures of Indian art — Hopi Kachina dolls, Navajo blankets and silver jewelry, Zuni pottery vessels, and hand-carved Makah totem poles are some examples — and, if possible, visit a museum or Indian center to appreciate the fine quality of the *real* artifacts.

Experiment with some of these crafts yourself to display in your exhibit:

CLAY POTS AND JARS

Use the "pinch" or "coil" method and decorate in bright colors with tempera paints. To make pinch pots, start with a small ball of clay. Insert both thumbs in the center and pinch all around until a pot is formed. For the coil method, flatten out a ball of clay for the base. Then roll out some more clay into a long "snake" and wind it around the base, gradually building up the sides. Dampen your fingers and smooth the inside of the pot to hold it together.

SANDPAINTING

Draw a picture on a box lid or cardboard food tray. Brush glue onto one small area at a time, then sprinkle with colored sand (dyed with tempera paint and water). Tap the picture to remove the excess sand, keeping each color in a separate jar. Add yarn, seashells, seeds, pebbles, sticks, or bits of eggshells for a variety of texture.

TOTEM POLES

Northwest Indians skillfully carved giant totem poles with animals, fish, birds, and objects from their everyday life to symbolize their own harmony with nature.

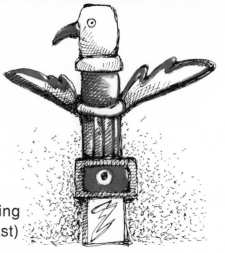

Make a model totem pole by stacking egg cartons or small boxes, corks, or spools on top of each other, adding cardboard tube wings and construction paper feathers and other features. Crayon or paint on colorful totem figures:

Thunderbird — Indian tribal crest
Beaver — lives near water
Paddle — transportation
Deer — hunting, food, and clothing
Flame — campfire, potlatch (feast)
Handclasp — friendship

Games

On cold winter nights Indian children sat around the fire listening while their fathers told them legends of their beginnings and ancestral heroes.

Often games followed the storytelling, and hoop-rolling and top-racing contests were among the favorites. Zuni, Hopi, and Navajo Indians played with tops called *nimitchie* (dancers) and flicked them with leather laces to speed them on.

Here are some other authentic Indian games from various tribes:

COMANCHE BALL AND DARTS

One player rolls a soft ball down a steep incline while the others aim darts (a toothpick stuck in a cork with paper feathers) at the moving ball. Pebbles can take the place of darts. Players get 10 points for hitting the moving target.

PUEBLO SQUASH BLOSSOMS

Players spread out in an open area and throw and catch three or four "squash blossoms" (woven squares). The players can't move from their position but just try to catch whatever's in their reach. When all the squash blossoms have fallen to the ground, they are gathered up and the game begins again. (Directions for making squash blossoms, also called God's Eyes, are in the Christmas chapter, p. 97.

HAND GAME

Two sticks are marked with paint on one end. One player conceals the painted ends in his fists, arranging the sticks in one of these three possible combinations:

color — right side   color — left side   color — both sides

The other player tries to guess which way the sticks are pointing.

LOTTO GAME

Did you know that twenty-seven of our states and many cities have Indian names? How many can you find on a map?

Make up a *lotto game* using these and other Indian words that have come into everyday use in our language:

powwow	moccasin	Tallahassee
skunk	syrup	Oklahoma
hammock	canoe	Cincinnati
wigwam	succotash	Oconomowoc
toboggan	chipmunk	Mississippi
cactus	Wisconsin	Cheyenne

To make the lotto boards and playing cards, divide sheets of cardboard into four or six squares and write a *different* Indian word on each square. Using construction paper, make a set of word cards corresponding to each lotto board.

To play the game:

1. Deal out the boards, one to each player, and place all the cards face down in a pile.
2. Take turns drawing a card, either matching it to a square on your board or returning it to the bottom of the pile.
3. The first player to cover his board is the winner.

FEATHER GRAB

Everyone dances around a feather stuck into a ball of clay. One person beats on a drum, and when the music stops, the dancer closest to the feather stoops down and tries to pluck it out with his teeth, keeping his hands behind his back. Put a new feather in for each round (either real or paper).

OMAHA PLUM STONE GAME

YOU NEED:
- 5 plum pits or small stones
- felt markers
- a basket or wooden bowl
- 100 counters (Indians used stalks of grass; you can use sticks or toothpicks)

YOU DO:
1. Clean and dry the pits.
2. Paint 3 pits black on one side (leaving the natural color on the other side). On each of the remaining two stones, draw a crescent moon on one side and a star on the others. Place all the stones in the bowl or basket.
3. Two players sit opposite one another and draw lots to see who starts.
4. Each player, holding both sides of the bowl, flips the stones in the air. He scores points according to how the stones land *in the basket.*

2 moons + 3 whites (natural) or 3 blacks = 10 points
2 stars + 3 blacks or 3 whites = 10 points
1 moon + 1 star + 3 whites = 5 points
1 moon + 1 star + 3 blacks = 5 points
(No other combinations count.)

As long as you keep scoring points, your turn continues. The object is to win 50 points (you might choose less); each player keeps his own score with the counters.

OCTOBER

COLUMBUS DAY OCTOBER 12

Christopher Columbus, an Italian mapmaker and sailor, spent many years seeking money to fulfill his dream of finding a short-cut to Asia. Finally, at the age of forty-six, he set sail, thanks to King Ferdinand and Queen Isabella of Spain. Thinking he had reached the Indies, Columbus and his crew accidentally discovered America in 1492. He called the natives who came to meet his exploring party "Indios," the Spanish word for Indians.

Charting the Voyage

Chart Columbus's voyage on construction paper, using crayons, glue, scissors, and toothpicks. Glue on the Niña, Pinta, and Santa Maria, the three ships that brought Columbus and eighty-nine other adventurers to the New World. Show their route from Spain to the Canary Islands and, finally, the landing at San Salvador in the Bahamas.

Spyglass

Columbus couldn't spot the North Star with a telescope because he set sail over a hundred years *before* the telescope was invented. You can be a modern sailor with a make-believe spyglass. Just insert a small cardboard tube into a larger one. For a nautical look, you can paint or cover the tubes with foil first. Can you spy land?

Make Your Own Compass

YOU NEED: a darning needle   YOU DO: 1. Rub the ends of the magnet across the needle about fifty times, always going in the same direction. This magnetizes the needle.
                 a magnet
                 a cork
                 a dish or bowl of water

2. Push the needle into the cork and lay it in a small dish of water. Try moving the cork in different directions. No matter which way you turn the cork, the needle will always point . . . north? south? east? west? Can you find out why?

Finding North

If you are Columbus's navigator and have forgotten your compass, don't panic . . . there's still another way to find North!

1. Go outdoors on a sunny day at 12 noon (1 p.m. if it is Daylight Saving Time) and place a large stick into the ground. Can you see a shadow? It will be pointing north.

2. Run a string along the line of the shadow to guide you in finding north after sundown.

3. When night comes, look up in the sky in the direction of your guideline. Do you see a group of stars in the shape of a ladle? It's called the Little Dipper and the bright star in its handle is the North Star. It never changes position in the sky, and that is why, for centuries, sailors have used the North Star to guide their course.

Look up at the sky the second week in October. Are you surprised to think that it looks the *same* as Columbus saw it five hundred years ago!

HALLOWEEN OCTOBER 31

Although Halloween takes its name from "All Hallow's Evening" (the night before the Christian festival of All Saints' Day), it is not itself a religious holiday. Halloween is a time of mischief when ghosts and witches are likely to wander about. This nightly haunting began in ancient Britain when the Druids lit fires on the hillsides and dressed in grotesque costumes and masks to scare away winter's evil spirits. You, too, can dress up like a spooky goblin for your wanderings on All Hallow's Evening!

Costumes
Make Your Own!

Large grocery bags, worn-out sheets and pillowcases, old clothes and a few trimmings are all you need to make costumes for trick-or-treat night or a Halloween party. Wigs, moustaches, scarves, hats, capes, and eyeglass frames are good basic props to have on hand.

WITCH

To the usual black pointed hat attach paper strips or an old stringy mop for straggly hair. Cut a cloak from crepe paper or cloth and put on dark socks and long black gloves . . . or tape on pointed paper fingernails. Glue or tie on an ugly crooked nose and even a paper wart . . . and don't forget your broomstick!

SKELETONS

Attach white adhesive or reflecting tape to dark clothing or a paper bag to look like bones.

ANIMAL

Draw spots or stripes on a bag or pillowcase with felt markers or paints. Use pipe cleaners or straws for whiskers and braided yarn, rope, or old nylons for a tail. Tape on claws made from Styrofoam food trays. Glue or staple floppy or pointed ears to a headband, or tie the tips of a paper bag together with a string and cut a large opening for your face. Some children like to have their own faces painted to match the animal's body!

OTHER IDEAS

Be a ghost, a pirate, an astronaut, a gypsy, a clown, a princess, a bride; Batman, Wolf Man, Dracula, Frankenstein, or some other monster; a hockey, baseball, or football player; Mother Goose, a storybook or comic strip character.

A *large box* with one hole cut in the top for your head and two armholes on the sides will make an original costume; come as a TV set, a robot, a box of your favorite cereal, a playing card, a pinball machine, or a spooky tree.

Masks

Turn a paper food tray, a plate, or a sheet of construction paper into a mask. Draw and cut out features; decorate with crayons, yarn, and paper and cloth scraps. Punch a hole on each side of the mask to tie on yarn (or staple on some elastic).

For a sturdier mask, first make a form out of clay and cover it with plastic wrap. Then lay several layers of papier mâché over the entire area (see p. 14, "Welcome Pineapple," for papier-mâché directions). When hardened, pull off the paper mask and paint it to go with your costume. You can still use the soft clay for another project.

Trick-or-Treat Bags

The trick-or-treat custom goes back to the seventeenth century when the Irish went from door to door collecting for a feast. Today, many "beggars" take both "treat bags" and UNICEF cans on their visits around the neighborhood.

For your own collection of goodies, decorate a grocery bag with paper cutouts, crepe paper, and felt markers. A shopping bag will have a ready-made handle for you, but if you don't have one handy, punch two holes, reinforce with tape, and add a handle of rope, ribbon, or heavy string.

Plan a Halloween party . . . and make it as scary and spooky as you can! BOO!

Party Games

SPIDER WEB

Playing this outdoors is better, but use your basement if it rains. The players are given a ball of string, a different color for each. At a signal each person ties the end of his string to an object, such as a tree trunk. Then he starts unraveling the string — winding it around the fence post, under the swing set, around a bush, and over the clothesline, etc. — until all the string is used and a "spider web" appears! See who can be first to wind his string back into a ball again!

WITCHES RELAY

Divide into two teams and give the first in line a broom and a pair of rolled socks. Each player, in turn, "sweeps" the socks to the finish line and back until one team wins.

SPOOKY SOUNDS

One player (the Witch) sits blindfolded with her back to the group (the Goblins). Each Goblin, one by one, creeps up close to the wicked Witch and makes a spooky sound, disguising his voice to fool her. The witch then tries to identify the Goblin and when she guesses correctly, she changes places with the Goblin whom she caught. The Goblin must then become the wicked Witch!

PUMPKIN RELAY

The first player on each team is given a crayon and runs to his goal line, where he finds a large piece of paper taped to the floor. He must draw a big circle, run back to the line, and give the crayon to the next player, who adds the stem. The remaining players, in turn, draw on the features of a jack-o-lantern. (You could also draw a witch, a black cat or a skeleton, etc.) See which team makes its picture the quickest . . . the funniest . . . the ugliest . . . or whatever you choose.

"Halloween Night"

Words & Music by Nancy Mack

It's al-most Hal-lo-ween night, when wit-ches fly high up in the sky.

"Oh, what a spook-y sight," say I. The ghosts are call-ing out "Boo!" and

gob-lins scream, Jack o' lan-terns gleam, but I'm not scared, are you?

Pumpkin Decorating

Put an old-fashioned **JACK-O'-LANTERN** with a glowing candle on your doorstep to greet your Halloween "beggars."

"ADD-ON" VEGETABLE FACES

For a pumpkin which will last for days, add on the eyes, ears, nose, and mouth, instead of carving them in the usual way. Using toothpicks, stick on carrots, cucumbers, radishes, small gourds, raisins, or other fall vegetables and fruits. You might add straw, yarn, leaves, or shreds of crepe paper for the hair and top it with a funny hat.

A CONTEST

Get together with your neighborhood for a pumpkin decorating contest. Announce that there'll be ribbons for the most original, the funniest, the prettiest, etc. Then don't be surprised when such imaginative entries as Cutie Cucumber, The Gourd Girls, Sinbad Squash the Sailor, and Pumpkin Postman appear.

What Halloween Party would be complete without a **HAUNTED HOUSE?** Here are two versions. The first spook house, where children go *without* a blindfold, is only a little scary and best for preschoolers.

1. Tell your friends that they're going on a visit to the House of the Wicked Witch.
2. Lead them into a slightly darkened room where they must crawl through a long tunnel (made from large, open boxes, chairs, or small tables draped with a sheet); be sure to tape spiders, bats, or other spooky cutouts to the sheets. Flash the lights on and off, occasionally focusing a beam on one of the horrible objects to cast shadows inside the tunnel.
3. Next, have them climb over a "bridge" (a chair or stepladder) and then finally arrive at the Witch's House (a large packing box or covered table).
4. A knock at the "door" brings forth the Witch herself, busy stirring her brew . . . claws of a buzzard, tongue of a tarantula, wings of a bat, eye of a newt.
5. Surprise! The caldron is filled with spicy apple cider or punch for all to enjoy.

For older children who aren't afraid to have their eyes covered, make the Spook House *really* scary . . .

1. Blindfold your friends and lead them, one at a time, through the Hall of Horrors. Let eerie sounds fill the air (made by a record player or tape recorder played on the wrong speed or by cackly voices and high-pitched screeches). Make spooky hangings to rub against their faces (an old mop, crepe paper skeletons, spiders on strings).
2. Place their hands into bowls of slimy objects, like peeled grapes (eyeballs), wet noodles (intestines), chilled, greased cauliflower (brains), or rubber gloves filled with wet sand (a dead man's hand).
3. Tickle their arms with a feather and tell them it's a spider or a bat.

Haunted Houses

Pumpkin Seeds

If you carved your pumpkin, don't throw away the seeds. Wash and dry them thoroughly and recycle them!

Roast them: Pour ¼ cup of oil on a cookie sheet and spread out the seeds, coating them well. Bake in a 350° oven until lightly brown. Drain on a paper towel, sprinkle with salt, and store in a covered jar for a tasty snack.

String them together using a needle and thread to make bracelets, necklaces, and other jewelry. Leave plain or dye first with food coloring.

Combine them with other seeds (melon, bird, fruit, etc.) to make a mosaic. Draw a picture, put glue on one section at a time and fill in with seeds. For a "kitchen collage" add bits of cereal, rice, dried peas or beans, macaroni, or popcorn. A boxlid or a cardboard food tray will provide a perfect base and a ready-made frame.

A GAME

Race! Each player is given 5 to 10 pumpkin seeds in a paper cup, a small dish, and a straw. At the "go" signal, everyone tries to pick up a seed and transfer it from the cup to the dish by sucking in on the straw. The first person to move all of his seeds wins. For older players add more seeds — or substitute an egg carton for the saucer and have the players drop a seed into each section.

GUESSING GAME

And finally, an old favorite: Fill a jar with seeds and have the family guessing contest — then count the seeds together to see who came the closest!

Party Treats

WITCHES' BREW (Hot Apple Cider)

In a large saucepan, combine 2 quarts apple cider, 3 sticks cinnamon, and 1 teaspoon each of whole cloves, whole allspice, and chopped candied ginger. Heat to boiling and then reduce heat and simmer for 10 minutes. Pour through a strainer before serving. Garnish with a stick of cinnamon.

SPOOKY SWEETS

First bake and ice cupcakes or cookies (use orange or chocolate frosting) or make ice cream balls. Then decorate to resemble black cats, witches, or goblins with licorice, corn candy, gumdrops, raisins, chocolate chips or sprinkles.

HAPPY PUMPKIN CAKE

Bake a cake in a round layer pan. Tint the frosting orange by adding red and yellow food coloring mixed together. Border the cake and draw on a broad smile with chocolate coconut. Use candy corn for the teeth and eyes and licorice for a stem.

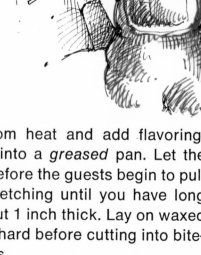

For generations, bobbing for apples in a giant tub or eating marshmallows dangling from a string in a doorway have been Halloween party favorites. To borrow some other ideas from great-grandma's time, you might want to try these recipes.

TAFFY PULL

YOU NEED:
- 2 cups sugar
- ⅔ cup water
- 4 tablespoons butter
- 2 teaspoons cream of tartar
- 1 teaspoon vanilla or mint flavoring

YOU DO:

1. Mix the sugar, water, butter, and cream of tartar in a saucepan and place over *low* heat, stirring constantly until the sugar is dissolved.
2. *Increase heat* (do not stir) until a *firm* ball can be made by dropping a dab of the mixture into cold water.
3. Remove from heat and add flavoring. Then pour into a *greased* pan. Let the taffy cool before the guests begin to pull it. Keep stretching until you have long pieces about 1 inch thick. Lay on waxed paper until hard before cutting into bite-sized pieces.

CANDIED APPLES

YOU NEED:
2 cups sugar
½ cup light corn syrup
¾ cup water
⅛ teaspoon salt
¼ teaspoon food coloring
¼ teaspoon cinnamon or mint flavoring
6 skewer sticks
6 apples
6 paper baking cups

YOU DO:
1. Pour sugar, syrup, water, and salt into a saucepan and place over medium heat, *stirring constantly* until mixture comes to a boil.
2. Continue cooking without stirring until syrup forms a hard ball when a bit is dropped into cold water.
3. Remove saucepan from stove and place in a pan of very hot water. Add coloring and flavoring, stirring slightly.
4. Now stick a skewer into each apple at stem end and quickly dip the apple into the syrup, swirling it several times.
5. Place each candied apple in a paper baking cup or on waxed paper until it hardens.

POPCORN BALLS

YOU NEED:
1½ cup popcorn kernels
1 package orange gelatin
1 cup sugar
1 cup corn syrup
orange food coloring

YOU DO:
1. First pop the corn.
2. Mix together the gelatin, sugar, and syrup and a few drops of food coloring. Heat to a full boil.
3. Pour the mixture over the popcorn, stirring well to thoroughly coat. Let cool.
4. Now butter your hands and shape the popcorn into small balls. Place on waxed paper for several hours; then wrap in cellophane or small sandwich bags and tie with a colorful ribbon. Decorate the bags, if you wish.

NOVEMBER

THANKSGIVING

The first Thanksgiving was a day of prayers, games, and feasting shared by the Pilgrims and Indians. The Pilgrims were grateful to have survived that long, hard winter in Massachusetts and were thankful for good health and an abundant harvest. They were particularly grateful to the Indians for teaching them to plant crops, prepare food, and adapt to their new surroundings.

Even today, the tone of Thanksgiving is one of sharing, as American families of all ethnic and religious backgrounds gather for a joyous celebration.

Let's go back to 1620 and recreate the Pilgrims' journey and the tiny village where they spent their first Thanksgiving. Here are two ways — both three-dimensional — to make these historic events come alive.

Plymouth Village

Reconstruct Plymouth Village as it looked over 350 years ago.

1. Using cardboard or a large box lid for a base, tape on Indian tepees and split-log houses. Make the tepees from twigs and brown paper (grocery bags are good).
   For log houses, cover small cardboard boxes or milk cartons with Popsicle sticks; add a thatched roof made from grass or crepe paper strips and a clay chimney (see Lincoln Log Cabin, p. 24).
2. Put the village in its natural setting with trees, bushes, and cornstalks, and surround with a stockade fence.
3. Tiny figures can be made from construction paper or by dressing up wooden clothespins or spools.
4. You might want to include an outdoor cooking area with a miniature Thanksgiving table laden with "food" made from clay or fun dough.

Salt Relief Map

Try making a Salt Relief Map showing the Pilgrim's trip from Plymouth, England, to Plymouth, Massachusetts.

YOU NEED:
salt mixture (2 cups salt, 2 cups flour, 1⅓ cups water)
a large piece of cardboard or a box lid
tempera paints
felt marker
brush
clay
walnut shells
toothpicks
paper

YOU DO:

1. Blend the salt and flour together and then slowly add the water, stirring until smooth. Spread onto the cardboard or box lid.
2. Build up the New England and the "old" England shores, leaving a flat area for the Atlantic Ocean in the center.
3. After your map has dried, paint the land and sea areas labeling the ocean and the Plymouths. Mark the number of miles and days the Pilgrims traveled across the Atlantic.
4. Sail the "Mayflower" (made from a walnut shell, a dab of clay, toothpicks, and paper sails) on the open sea, and place "Plymouth Rock" and an Indian settlement along the "rugged" coastline.
5. You might add the names of towns in the New England that the Pilgrims and later settlers named after the English villages that they left behind: Falmouth, Portsmouth, Dover, Southampton, and many others.

Indian and Pilgrim Flip Dolls

YOU NEED:
- a shoebox with its lid
- construction paper
- scissors
- glue
- cardboard
- crayons
- yarn
- felt or flannel

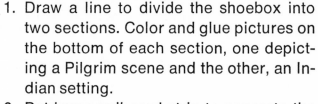

YOU DO:

1. Draw a line to divide the shoebox into two sections. Color and glue pictures on the bottom of each section, one depicting a Pilgrim scene and the other, an Indian setting.
2. Put in a cardboard strip to separate the sections.
3. Draw and cut out two cardboard flip dolls with a boy on one side and a girl on the other.
4. Color in their faces and add yarn for hair. Glue felt or flannel on the rest of the body.
5. Make felt doll clothes (they will stick to the flannel) and store them in the appropriate section of the box.

The Pilgrim girl might wear a long skirt, a petticoat and apron, stiff white collar and cuffs, a cotton bonnet.

The Pilgrim boy could have knee-length breeches, long stockings, a doublet (short jacket), buckled shoes, and a tall hat or knitted cap. (Remember, the Pilgrims did not always dress in the traditional black . . . they wore bright colors just as you do!)

The Indian girl might wear a fringed deerskin skirt and vest, beads, and a feathered headband.

The Indian boy could have a loincloth or cape made of animal skins, a headband, and a quiver with bow and arrows. (For Indian doll clothes, you could use brown wrapping paper fringed on the edges and backed with felt.)

Games

Games also played an important part in the three-day Thanksgiving celebration. Vines were used for jumping rope, a tree bough for playing limbo, and round seeds for marble shooting. Although the pilgrims and Indians also enjoyed wrestling, marksmanship, hide-and-seek, and foot races, you might welcome quieter games after *your* big turkey feast!

a pilgrim jumped on a pickle

WORD GAMES

See how many words can be made from the word "Thanksgiving."

Make a funny game telling how the Pilgrims came to New England. Following the alphabet, each player in turn adds the name of a silly kind of transportation. For example, first player: "The Pilgrims came over on an *Aardvark.*" Second player: "The Pilgrims came over on an *Aardvark* and a *Butterfly.*" Third player: "The Pilgrims came over on an *Aardvark,* a *Butterfly,* and a *Cucumber.*" And so forth.

FEATHER GAME

Make an Indian headband or a turkey with construction-paper feathers and write a "stunt" on the back of each one. As each player pulls off a feather, he must act out the stunt.

Some Silly Stunts:

1. Walk around the room balancing a penny on your forehead.
2. Spell your name backwards and then pronounce it.
3. Walk on your knees holding your ankles behind you.
4. Imitate a tightrope walker.
5. Twirl around four times and when you stop, stand on one foot.
6. Sing one song while another person is singing a completely different one.
7. See how fast you can say "Rubber Baby Buggy Bumpers."

Thanksgiving Feast

Did you know that there were more Indians than Pilgrims at the first Thanksgiving feast and that it lasted three whole days? Leek salad, coarse wheat-flour biscuits, and dried gooseberries were on the menu . . . but don't despair. They also shared many of the foods that we still enjoy today: cranberries, cornbread, succotash, squash, pumpkin pie, and, of course, stuffed turkey with all the trimmings.

TURKEY STUFFING

Depending on where you live, your family probably has a typical recipe for turkey dressing. Why not try a variation from another part of the country?

Begin with a *quart* of basic stuffing.

For:

New England Oyster Dressing, add 1 cup chopped drained oysters.

Midwest Sausage Dressing, omit the salt and add ⅓ pound bulk pork sausage crumbled and browned.

Southern Pecan Dressing, add ⅔ cup coarsely chopped pecans.

Far West Apple-Raisin Dressing, add 1 cup finely chopped apples and ¼ cup raisins.

Present your turkey "in style" with these original fruit combinations:

CRANBERRY "MAYFLOWER" BOATS

1. Fill a peach or pear half with cranberry sauce, one for each guest.
2. For a sail, poke a toothpick through a carrot shaving or a lemon or orange peel and stick it in the peach.

ORANGE-CUP "TURKEYS"

1. Cut oranges in half, scoop out the pulp, and mix it with cranberry sauce. Then fill each orange cup for the turkey body.
2. For the turkey's head, use toothpicks to attach a radish, spiced apple, cherry tomato, or kumquat. Raisins can be added for the features, and carrot sticks or celery tops for the tail.

What other festive foods can you create?

CENTERPIECES

Display your three-dimensional village or salt map as a centerpiece, surrounded by Tater Turkeys or Pumpkin Pilgrims. Use a sweet potato or a pumpkin for the head or body. Decorate with Thanksgiving trimmings, such as cranberries, marshmallows, and raisins, held in place with toothpicks. Make turkey feathers or Pilgrim hats from construction paper.

Walnut "Mayflowers," paper turkeys or wigwams could serve as placecards to match your centerpiece.

When the pilgrim hunters went out seeking geese for the dinner, to their surprise, they found turkeys instead! No doubt that's why turkeys and Thanksgiving are still an inseparable pair. Here are some **TURKEYS YOU CAN'T EAT** . . .

1. Place your hand on a piece of paper and trace around it. Can you finish the turkey by adding a wattle and feet? Color in the feathers and features.
2. Glue or staple two small paper plates together for the body (or stuff a grocery bag). Add a head, feet, and feathers made from construction paper or comic pages.
3. Bend a wire coat hanger into the shape of a turkey. Cover with an old silk stocking and then glue on features as above.

Use yarn to hang each turkey from a doorway, a light fixture, or a window, or attach *all* the turkeys to a wire hanger for a mobile.

Finish the day with some

Holiday Songs

THE PUMPKIN RAN AWAY (to the tune of "Farmer in the Dell")
The Pumpkin ran away
    (Cranberry — 2nd verse)
    (Turkey — 3rd verse)
Before Thanksgiving Day
Said he, "They'll make a pie out of me
             (sauce — 2nd verse)
             (roast — 3rd verse)

If I decide to stay!

A FUNNY BIRD (make up your own tune)
The turkey is a funny bird
His head goes wobble, wobble.
And all he says is just one word . . .
Gobble, Gobble, Gobble,
Gobble, Gobble, Gobble.

DECEMBER

CHANUKAH

Chanukah is the eight-day Festival of Lights. Each night one more candle on the menorah is lit until all eight are burning brightly. This recalls the "miracle of the lamp," when the victorious Hebrew army returned to worship in its damaged temple to find only enough oil for the "eternal light" to burn for *one* day . . . but, instead, it lasted for eight — until a messenger brought more. Today's families play games and exchange gifts on each of the eight nights of Chanukah.

For a simple but attractive menorah, flatten a ball of clay into a circle about an inch thick. Cut it in half and join together. Poke eight candle holes in the base and one at the top for the Shamus, the candle that lights the others.

Menorah

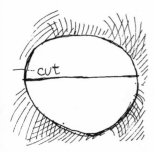

The hero of the Chanukah story is Judah Maccabee, who for three years led his tiny band of soldiers against the powerful Syrian army of Emperor Antiochus IV. The Maccabees' clever strategy was to set up a "dummy camp" to fool the Syrians. They then hid in the neighboring hills in order to surround the enemy when they attacked the "camp."

Mural

Draw a mural depicting the story, using such figures and symbols as the temple with an altar, an oil lamp, Judah Maccabee, army shields with Star of David insignias, Antiochus, and the dummy camp.

Chanukah Game

You could also reenact these early days with a game. The leader, Judah Maccabee, stands in his camp, a circle drawn on the ground; the other players, the Syrians, tease him by running in and out of the circle trying not to get caught. Judah may not leave his camp until he tags a Syrian; then that player becomes the next leader.

Chanukah Treat

Whether you're having a holiday party or just a family dinner, no Chanukah meal is complete without **POTATO LATKES**!

YOU NEED:
- 4 potatoes, grated
- 1 egg
- 1 small onion (optional)
- salt
- 1 tablespoon flour

YOU DO: Mix all ingredients well; then drop by large rounded spoonfuls onto a hot skillet (greased generously with melted margarine). Fry on both sides until brown. Serve piping hot with sour cream or applesauce.

Dreidels

Dreidels make festive party favors or decorations. A dreidel is a four-sided wooden or plastic top . . . but you can easily make one out of a square cardboard box and a pencil. There is a Hebrew letter on each side.

נ nes ג gadol ה haya ש sham

These letters begin the words that mean "a great miracle happened there."

Dreidels are most often enjoyed as a game. Who can spin theirs the longest? Which letter will land on top?

Chant this typical Chanukah song:

I have a little dreidel
I made it out of clay
And when it's dry and ready
Then dreidel I shall play.

CHRISTMAS DECEMBER 25

December, with the promise of Christmas, is a time of excitement and anticipation for Christians everywhere.

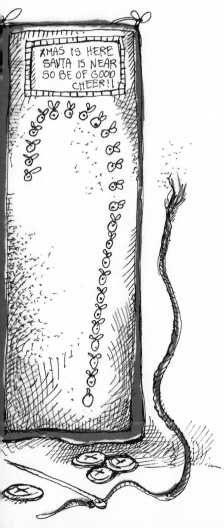

XMAS IS HERE
SANTA IS NEAR
SO BE OF GOOD
CHEER!!

Advent Calendar

One way to help mark off the days and days of waiting is through this homemade *Advent Calendar*.

YOU NEED: a long strip of felt or any heavy material
25 buttons
needle
yarn
paper
pen

YOU DO:
1. Write a poem about the coming of Christmas and glue it to the top of the felt strip.
2. Tie on the 25 buttons with yarn bows.
3. Glue or sew a pocket on the back to hold the buttons as you remove them.
4. Untie one button each day, beginning on December 1.

As a variation, the buttons could be arranged in different holiday shapes, such as a tree, bell, candy cane, or whatever you like.

Crèche

The birthday of Christ is celebrated in many different ways according to the individual traditions of each family. Many families display a crèche, often handing it down from generation to generation. Small children wait impatiently for the exciting moment when the nativity scene is set up in its place of honor.

You can create your own crèche by making simple cardboard or fun-dough figures of Mary, Joseph, and the infant Jesus. You might also include the three Wise Men, the shepherds, and the animals who came to the stable. (To make dough figures, see cookie ornaments, p. 99.)

Christmas Cards

Get into the holiday spirit by starting early on your Christmas cards. Beginning with colorful construction paper, try some of these ideas:

1. *Draw a holiday picture* using crayons, paints, or felt markers. Add glitter, if you wish.
2. *Glue on cutouts* (from old Christmas cards, wrapping paper, magazines, and newspapers) and border with yarn, ribbon, rickrack, or braid.
3. *Print a design* using tempera paints and carved vegetable slices (potatoes, carrots, etc.).

Look back to Valentine's Day for other ways to make cards (p. 19)! And don't forget to make one for Santa!

HOLIDAY HANG-UPS

Put the cards *you* receive on "display" to enjoy throughout the holiday season.

Cut a holiday shape (tree, wreath, stocking) from cardboard and cover it with foil or construction paper. Tape on your favorite cards or simply put them on a long ribbon or strip of felt. *Tip*: If you attach your cards with a small piece of *rolled* masking tape on the back, they can be easily removed later.

String a clothesline or ribbon across a doorway, mantle or window and clip on the cards with decorated clothespins or paper clips. Cards can also be glued to paper snowflakes and hung from the line.

Old-Fashioned Trees

Perhaps the earliest decorated Christmas tree was inspired by Martin Luther (around A.D. 1500). Legend tells that after returning home from a walk one Christmas Eve, he suggested that his children light candles on their tree to look like the heavenly stars.

The first written account of the decorated tree, about a hundred years later, described colorful paper roses, apples, wafers, gold foil, and sweets.

Recapture the warmth of the old-fashioned Christmas tree of great-grandmother's day by replacing store-bought ornaments and tinsel with calico bows and strings of popcorn and cranberries.

Everyday objects, such as knitted mittens, metal cookie cutters, or cornhusk, yarn and other small dolls can be tied to the branches with colorful yarn or ribbon.

You can also drape the tree with garlands of candy canes, miniature paper stockings, bells, and "ice cream cones" with cotton tops to keep that homespun touch.

If Santa had visited your house a hundred years ago, he might have found a **CANDY BASKET** hanging on your tree!

Make a cone of wrapping paper or foil. Line with brightly colored tissue paper or paper lace doilies. Add a handle and fill with candies or homemade cookies.

Santa might be tempted by these **COOKIE ORNAMENTS** but they aren't for eating!

1. To make the dough, mix 4 cups flour, 1 cup salt, and 1½ cups water and knead thoroughly. Add more water, if too dry.
2. Form shapes and figures on foil or wax paper, or roll out and cut with holiday cookie cutters.
3. Push in sequins, buttons, or small beads, if you wish.
4. Poke a hole with a straw or insert a paper clip for hanging on the tree.
5. Bake at 200° for 1 hour.
6. Paint on designs after baking and shellac, if you wish.

To borrow another Early American custom, use knitting needles, fruits, and greens to create **MINIATURE TREES** for the tabletop.

Stack a row of apples onto a large knitting needle and surround with other apples (attached with toothpicks) in a pyramid shape.

For a newer version, stack a grapefruit, orange and lemon (the largest on the bottom) onto the needle and attach cranberries, gumdrops and marshmallows for ornaments.

OTHER HANDMADE ORNAMENTS

Whether you choose an old-fashioned tree or a more modern one, there are many more ornaments that you can easily make by recycling odds and ends.

Clothespin. Paint or dress clothespins to look like soldiers, dolls, or animals and clip them right to the branches.

Spool. Write each person's name on a painted spool or decorate it to look like a drum. Glue two toothpicks across the top for drumsticks.

Egg carton. Make holiday bells from egg carton sections and paint them in bright colors; for clappers, attach minimarshmallows or gumdrops to pipe cleaners.

Tissue paper. Glue holiday shapes of colored tissue paper or cellophane to black construction paper frames and hang these "stained glass" ornaments near a Christmas tree light or in a window.

Foil pans. Decorate shiny cutouts from disposable aluminum pie pans to reflect the bright colors and shapes around them.

Cardboard tubes. Fashion a Santa, a Wise Man, or an angel from a cardboard toilet tube. For the body, cover the tube with foil, felt, or cloth scraps. Then cut a hole in the bottom of an egg carton section and place it upside down on the tube for a collar. Draw the eyes, nose, and mouth on a Styrofoam, rubber, or Ping-Pong ball and glue the "head" onto the egg cup. Decorate with sequins, felt, glitter, braid, yarn, and, where appropriate, add pipe cleaner arms, a halo, etc.

Straw. Tie drinking straws and yarn together to form Christmas stars and snowflakes (cellophane straws or stirrers are particularly pretty).

God's Eye. An old Indian charm used to ward off evil spirits.
First cut two straws or sticks the same length and tie them together securely with yarn to form a cross. Beginning at the center, loop a length of yarn over one straw and completely around it, then under the next straw and completely around *it*. Repeating this process clockwise, stop ½ inch from the ends of the straws. Several colors of yarn make the prettiest designs.

Jar lid. Make two circles by tracing around a jar lid on felt, foil, or construction or wrapping paper. Glue one circle on the inside of the lid and decorate it with cutouts from old Christmas cards, magazines, wrapping paper, or family snapshots. Next cover the edge of the lid with braid, ribbon, or thick yarn. To hang, tape a loop of yarn or cord on the back of the jar lid and then glue on the remaining circle.

Felt Santa. Cut a circle from red felt and make a slit to the center; fold to form a cone and staple or sew together. Glue on a pink or brown felt circle for a face, a long white beard, and white felt or cotton for a fur-trimmed hat. Add black felt boots and eyes . . . and a red nose. Attach a loop for hanging.

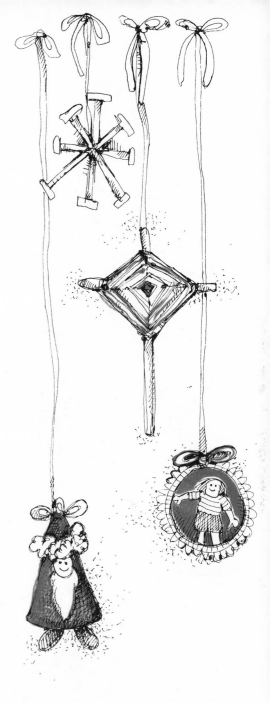

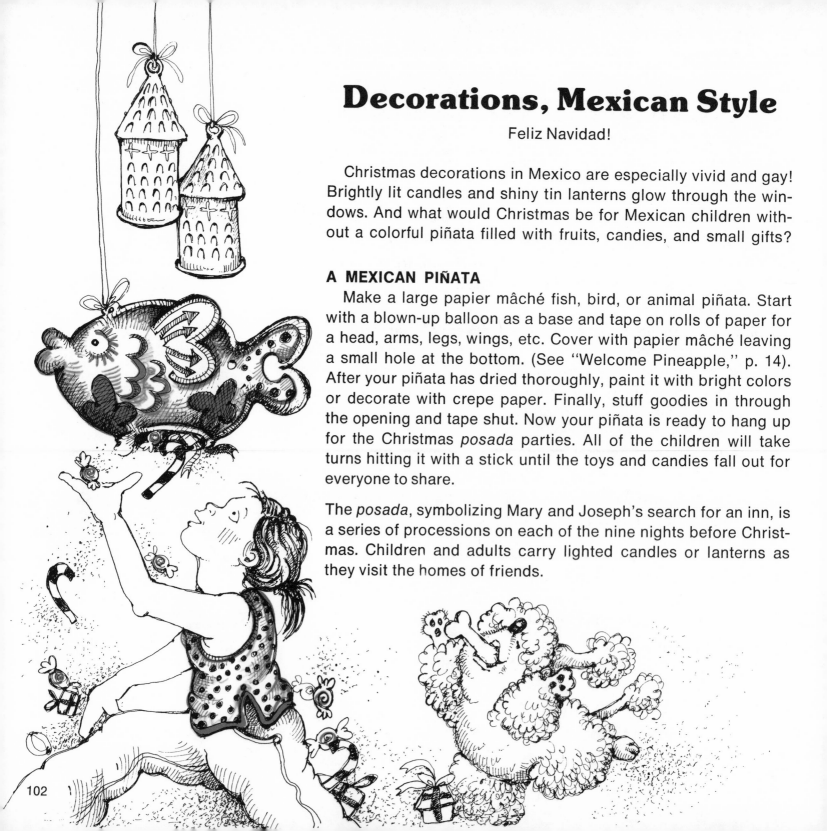

Decorations, Mexican Style

Feliz Navidad!

Christmas decorations in Mexico are especially vivid and gay! Brightly lit candles and shiny tin lanterns glow through the windows. And what would Christmas be for Mexican children without a colorful piñata filled with fruits, candies, and small gifts?

A MEXICAN PIÑATA

Make a large papier mâché fish, bird, or animal piñata. Start with a blown-up balloon as a base and tape on rolls of paper for a head, arms, legs, wings, etc. Cover with papier mâché leaving a small hole at the bottom. (See "Welcome Pineapple," p. 14). After your piñata has dried thoroughly, paint it with bright colors or decorate with crepe paper. Finally, stuff goodies in through the opening and tape shut. Now your piñata is ready to hang up for the Christmas *posada* parties. All of the children will take turns hitting it with a stick until the toys and candies fall out for everyone to share.

The *posada*, symbolizing Mary and Joseph's search for an inn, is a series of processions on each of the nine nights before Christmas. Children and adults carry lighted candles or lanterns as they visit the homes of friends.

CANDLES

For a mold, use cardboard juice cans, Styrofoam cups, or milk cartons of various sizes (with the tops cut off). Make a small hole in the bottom of each container for the wick and push through a piece of heavy string, knotting it underneath. Wind the other end of the string around a pencil or straw and place it across the top of the mold. Next melt paraffin or pieces of old candles in a saucepan or coffee can. Add bits of crayons, if you wish, but stick to similar colors to avoid a muddy effect. Now pour a small amount of wax into the container and let it harden slightly before pouring in the rest. When the candle is hard (putting it in the refrigerator or outdoors will speed up the process), just peel away the container!

LANTERNS

YOU NEED: tin cans of various sizes (washed and with edges pinched smooth with pliers)
a hammer and nails
a short candle
an old towel

YOU DO:

1. Fill each can with water and place in the freezer until frozen solid.
2. Lay the can sideways on an old folded towel and, using a hammer and nail, pound holes all over the can in an interesting design (not too close to the bottom because the wax may drip out later).
3. Let the ice melt (in the kitchen sink) and put a low, round candle in each lantern. (Press down in a few drops of melted wax.)
4. Place the tin lantern in a shallow dish or pie tin.

For a home decoration or centerpiece, cluster several lanterns or candles together and surround with evergreen and holly, or poinsettias (*flores de noche buena*) as they do in Mexico.

103

Centerpieces

Here's a simple **GINGERBREAD HOUSE**: No baking is needed, just add on the treats!

YOU NEED:
cardboard
scissors
tape
pretzels
gumdrops
lollipops
candy canes
licorice
chocolate chips
sugar sprinkles, etc.

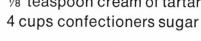

Sugar Frosting:
3 egg whites
⅛ teaspoon cream of tartar
4 cups confectioners sugar

YOU DO:

1. Cut out 4 sides, 2 roof pieces, and a chimney from cardboard; tape together and mount on a cardboard base or large tray.
2. To make the frosting, beat egg whites and cream of tartar until frothy. Gradually add sugar and beat until mixture holds soft peaks.
3. Spread frosting over the entire house. (Mix food coloring with a small part of the frosting for doors, windows and shutters, etc., if you wish.)
4. Press candy into the icing before it hardens. Make your candy house even more tempting with gumdrop bricks, chocolate chip shingles, and lots of sugar sprinkles.
5. To complete your centerpiece, frost the base and cover it with coconut "snow." Add candy-coated cobblestones, a marshmallow snowman, and surround with a lollipop or candy cane fence.

SANTA-IN-THE-CHIMNEY

YOU NEED: a large milk carton
construction paper
crayons or markers
an old sock
newspapers
cardboard tube
glue
scissors
string
trim: cotton, felt, buttons, cloth scraps

YOU DO:
1. Cover the milk carton with paper and color it to look like a brick chimney.
2. To make a Santa puppet, stuff an old sock with newspaper, push in a cardboard tube, and tie it securely with a string. Tape on rolled paper arms.
3. Sew or draw on a face, add cotton for a beard, and dress Santa in red with a black belt.
4. Stuff the chimney with paper to keep Santa steady, and toss a "sockful" of toys over his shoulder.

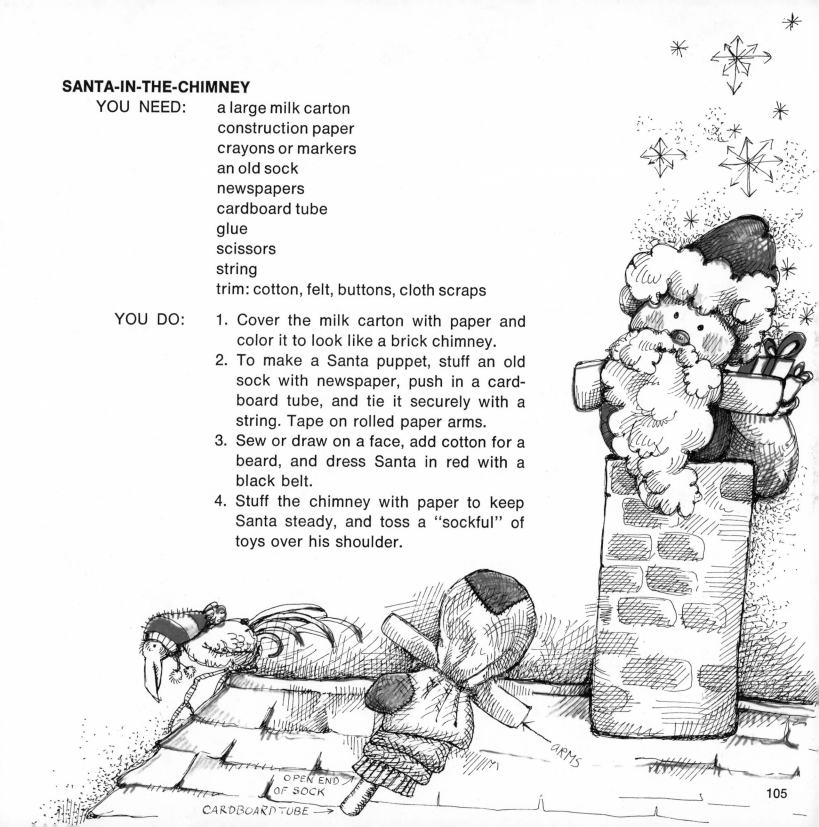

ARMS

OPEN END
OF SOCK

CARDBOARD TUBE →

Home Decorations

A combination of household items can make festive garlands for the tree, mantel, or staircase, or colorful wreaths for the door.

GARLANDS

Old-fashioned. Tie red velvet bows, pine cones (plain or spray-painted), nuts, or shiny apples with sprigs of greens and holly.

Snowflakes. Fold a square of white paper, Christmas wrap, or doily in half several times. Snip off the corners and cut out shapes along the edges. Unfold and string your "snowflakes."

Chains. Make a chain of metal "pop tops" (they can be sprayed or glittered) and weave yarn or cellophane through the holes. You can also cut up straws into different lengths and sew them together (vertically) with a needle and thread. Dangle small candy canes, tinsel, pompoms, beads, or other tiny ornaments from the chains.

WREATHS

Candy. Bend a hanger into a circle and tie or wire on wrapped candy. Tie a pair of scissors to the wreath with yarn or ribbon so that everyone can help himself! Candy can also be glued onto a round cardboard base or attached to a Styrofoam ring with wire or toothpicks.

Holly. Thread the end of a coat hanger through long strips of green crepe paper to give a full, leafy effect. Bend into a circle and attach "holly berries" made from covering butterbeans, marbles, buttons, or bottlecaps with red cellophane.

Find a "hideaway" in your home . . . behind a sofa, under a table, in a closet or a dark corner . . . or transform a large packing box into Santa's workshop. Cut out a door and windows and then decorate the box to look like the North Pole. "Stock" your workshop with scissors, tape, and lots of Christmas wrapping paper and ribbon. Take turns wrapping your presents so no one else will see your surprises!

Secret Wrapping Place

Holiday Cookie Exchange

Bake one kind of cookie and end up with a large assortment — sound impossible? Just invite several friends to your house for a cookie swap.

Ask each to bring a few dozen cookies made from a favorite holiday recipe and a container (a coffee can or an oatmeal box lined with waxed paper or foil) to decorate later.

As host you can set up a work table and supply tissue and construction paper, foil, scraps of wrapping paper, old Christmas cards, glue, and scissors. Include paper lace, braid, and sequins for finishing touches.

Each guest first decorates his cookie cannister, then fills it with a variety of goodies for a special gift for a teacher or friend.

You might ask all the "bakers" to bring along their recipe cards for everyone to copy.

An idea for *your* cookies: Add these festive touches to a basic sugar or butter cookie dough before baking —

CANDY CANES
Add red food coloring to half of the dough. Then divide the red and white dough into small balls and roll them into ropes. Twist pairs together to form a candy cane.

SUGAR PLUMS
Roll butter cookie dough (shaped in balls) in red and green colored sugar.

SNOWBALLS
Roll the cookie balls in shredded coconut.

Gifts

The widespread custom of giving Christmas gifts goes back to the three Wise Men, who traveled for many days to bring gold, frankincense, and myrrh to the Christ Child in the manger.

The early Christians believed that Jesus brought gifts on Christmas Eve while Saint Nicholas (the patron saint of children) brought them on the eve of December 6. Both traditions are combined in the custom of Santa Claus.

OLD-FASHIONED BREADS

You might begin your gift-making in the kitchen. Whip up several loaves of fruit cake or some "quick" breads (cranberry, banana, apricot, date and nut, etc.). Wrap each one in foil or plastic and cover or tie with gingham or calico for an old-fashioned touch.

For a tasty **SNACK MIX**, combine 1½ boxes of unsweetened, dry cereal, thin pretzels, and mixed nuts with 1 tablespoon seasoning salt, 1 tablespoon garlic salt, and 1 tablespoon Worchestershire sauce. Melt ½ cup margarine with ½ cup oil and pour over dry ingredients. Bake uncovered in a roasting pan for 1½ hours at 250°, stirring every 20 minutes.

Just a few homemade goodies or a single ornament make very thoughtful presents. Some families traditionally go out caroling on Christmas Eve and deliver these remembrances to their neighbors.

CARDBOARD MAILER

If you plan to send your gifts out-of-town, a cardboard tube from wrapping paper or paper toweling makes a sturdy *mailer*. Decorate with scraps of wrapping paper, stickers, paper snowflakes, ribbons, gold braid, and other holiday trim. Cover the tube with brown wrapping paper, tape the ends shut and add an address label.

Won't Grandpa be surprised to find an original drawing, tie, handkerchief, or greeting card rolled inside?

DECORATIVE GLASS JARS can be filled with cookies, candies, or a snack mix. First cut out holiday pictures from magazines, wrapping paper, or greeting cards. Dab glue on the *front* of the pictures and press inside a wide-mouthed jar. Brush acrylic paint over the cutouts; let dry thoroughly before filling. Tie on a bright ribbon to dress up your gift.

Stockings

No need to go out and buy a Christmas stocking. Its fun to create your own!

Make a newspaper pattern and use it to cut out two pieces of felt or other sturdy material. Sew the edges of the stocking together and decorate with felt cutouts and other trim. Don't forget to add your name.

Decorate an old knee sock or one of Dad's, the longer the better.

Knit a giant stocking, using large needles and thick yarn. It might last long enough to pass on to *your* own children — a new family tradition!

Rover and Kitty don't want to be forgotten! Trim and hang up a mesh onion or potato sack. Weave in yarn or ribbon patterns or sew on cloth cutouts.

A pop-up Santa is a **STOCKING STUFFER** that toddlers will especially love. Make Santa's head from an egg carton cup, cardboard disk or a small Styrofoam ball; glue on a red hat and cotton beard and attach it to one end of a straw. Put the other end of the straw through a hole in a paper cup and you'll have a Santa ready to peek out of a stocking.

Hang your stocking on your doorknob or bedpost so Mom and Dad can catch an extra forty winks.

A reminder to Santa: Besides small wrapped toys, be sure to tuck an orange or apple in the toe of the stocking and some packets of raisins, dry cereal, or other snacks to keep the kids going until their parents get up!

Christmas traditionally means mince pie and plum pudding! Here are some newer dishes to bring touches of color to your table.

CHRISTMAS FRUIT MOLD
Using red and green gelatin, follow the recipe on the box, substituting lime and raspberry sherbet for the cold water. Make one layer at a time and chill until partly firm before adding the second layer. Add cranberries, mandarin oranges, bananas, or nuts, if you wish.

TOMATO SANTA
Use broiled tomato slices for Santa's face and trim with a mashed potato "beard" and eyes, nose, and mouth made of peas.

VEGETABLE WREATH
Help Mom find a recipe for a spinach or broccoli soufflé. Bake in a ring mold set in a pan of water; unmold on a platter and surround with red cinnamon apples.

CHRISTMAS CAKES
Bake a cake in a round pan. Decorate to look like Santa's face or a church bell. For a tree, cut into a triangle; frost and trim with colored gumdrops or silver sprinkles.

Christmas Games

After the holiday dinner is over, the table must be cleared, the food put away, and the dishes washed and dried. Why not make a family game of the cleanup?

PICK-UPS
Write each chore on a slip of paper and drop it into a hat. Assign everyone a number, with #1 drawing first, etc.

With the chores behind you, here's a "drawing" game that's fun!

WHAT DID SANTA BRING?
Everyone pairs up and sits back to back. One player pulls an object from a Christmas stocking and describes it to his partner, who then tries to draw a picture of it. When all the pictures are finished, everyone tries to guess what they are and match them to the real objects.

After Christmas

OUTDOOR FEEDING STATION

Your Christmas tree can make a perfect outdoor feeding station. Just tie on some of these "delicacies."

Scoop out an orange or grapefruit and fill it with bacon fat, seeds, or nuts.

Spread peanut butter on a pine cone.

Put suet in a berry basket or tie it directly onto a branch. (Tell the butcher it's for the birds!)

YULE LOG (city style)

Saw off the end of your tree trunk and save it for *next* Christmas. Before burning it in the fireplace, have each member of the family touch the log and make a wish!

CHRISTMAS LEFTOVERS

Be sure to save your Christmas cards, bits of ribbon, braid, and wrapping paper for next year's ornaments, gifts, and decorations . . . and don't throw away those nice long wrapping paper tubes. Besides the Christmas mailing roll, they can later serve as a Fourth of July hobby horse, an Indian totem pole, a spyglass for Columbus Day, or a miniature Maypole.

POSTMARKS U.S.A.

Tape a large map of the United States on a wall where you can easily reach it. Then, as you receive Christmas cards, cut out the circular postmarks from the envelopes and tape or pin each postmark to its correct location on your map. Using a ruler, measure to find out how many miles each letter had to travel to reach your door! Save the stamps to make a colorful collage or to decorate a box.

BIBLIOGRAPHY

Arnold, Arnold. *The World Book of Children's Games.* Greenwich, Conn.: Fawcett Publications, 1972.

Barth, Edna. *Holly, Reindeer and Color*

———. *Lilies, Rabbits and Painted Eg*

Better Homes and Gardens (ed.). *Bett*

Childcraft Encyclopedia (ed.), Chicag

Compton's Encyclopedia (ed.). Chicag

Cosky, Evelyn. *Easter Eggs for Every*

Cram, Dorothy E. *Games for Special*

Creekmoore, Betsey. *Making Gifts fr*
1970.

Crocker, Betty. *Party Book.* New York:

Croft, Doreen J., and Hess, Robert
Boston: Houghton Mifflin Co., 197?

Early Years Magazine. Darien, Conn.:

Educational Insights, Inc. (ed.). *Creativ*

Fletcher, Alice C. *Indian Games and D*

Ginsburg, Marvell. *Holidays in the J*
Jewish Education, 1970.

K-3 Bulletin of Teaching Ideas and Mat

Keene, Frances W. *The Keene Party Bo*

Kohl, Marguerite, and Young, Frederica.

Mannings-Sanders, Ruth. *Festivals.* New

Maris, Irena. *Holiday Art.* Dansville, N.Y.

McSpadden, J. Walker. *The Book of H*

Morrow, Betty, and Hartman, Louis. *Je*

Newmarr, Dara. *The Teacher's Almana*

Peck, Ruth. *Teachers' Arts and Crafts*

Resources for Creative Preschool Te
Children, 1972.

Robbins, Ireene. *Elementary Teacher'*
N.Y.: Parker Publishing Co., 1970.

Rowe, Jeanne A. *An Album of Martin L*

Sattler, Helen R. *Recipes for Art and C*

Sechrist, Elizabeth H. *Red Letter Days*

Simon, Norma. *Hanukkah.* New York: T

Strose, Susanne. *Making Paper Flower*

Teacher Magazine. Greenwich, Conn.:

Van Hagen, Winifred; Dexter, Genevieve; and Williams, Jesse F. *Physical Education in the Elementary School.* Sacramento: California State Dept. of Education, 1951.

Vinton, Iris. *The Folkways Omnibus of Children's Games.* Harrisburg, Pa.: The Stackpole Co., 1970.

World Book Encyclopedia. Chicago: Field Enterprises, Inc., 1975.